I0060308

THE RECESSION
IS OVER

TIME TO GROW

Keith Churchouse

© May 2013

THE FOURTH CHURCHOUSE CHRONICLES©

FIRST EDITION

Acknowledgements

Esther Dadswell

The first acknowledgement always goes to Esther, my wife and fellow director, whose business and engineering prowess have been fundamental in allowing me to produce the text for these pages. Esther, your ability to process-drive work to volume levels is significant in lifting our business success.

I am also grateful for your unrelenting guidance in my continued writing.

Thank you for staying around.

I would not have taken the best part of my varying journeys without you.

Rosamund and Roger Churchouse

A common theme is emerging here in thanking you both for putting up with me.

It's been both fun and inspiring. Your wisdom and counsel are of great value.

The team at Guildford College

Thank you for helping me release time in my business by finding a top quality apprentice in the form of Mr Jack Bishop.

My translation team

My books have taken on a far more diverse life than I could have ever anticipated through the care, considered attention and help of my friends in Brazil, namely Suzana Chazan, and Valeria Haasper . My 'translation team' in this glorious country has helped me develop an international approach to my writing work. For this, I am truly grateful. I look forward to working with you all on our future projects together.

My loyal work friends and colleagues

To Gordon B, Steve W, Kevin L, Donald McN, Phil B, Marc C and the others I am always pleased to hear from.

ISBN 978-0-9573125-2-4

Further contact details and information can be found at www.the-recession-is-over.co.uk

No financial advice or legal advice of any description is offered or deemed to have been provided during the text of this book.

Some of the names, titles, sequencing, areas and dates have been amended to ensure that this work portrays a personal experience rather than those of individuals or companies. Any similarity to individuals and groups is purely coincidental. This book is also an expression of the personal opinion of the author and his view on the future of the economy, both national and global.

A donation will be made to the charity *Headway Surrey* for each book sold.

Headway Surrey supports people throughout Surrey with brain injuries, their families and carers, and promotes understanding of the implications of brain injury.

Registered Charity No: 1046863
www.headwaysurrey.org

To the guiding hands that have helped me with this book
Thank you to:

Fiona Cowan, Words That Work
Contact: wordsbird.wordpress.com

Graham Booth, Creation Booth
Contact: www.creationbooth.com

And finally my clients past, present and future

My warmest thanks go to you, without whom I would not have enjoyed my journey through business start-up, incubation, development, growth and successful maturity.

Thank you.

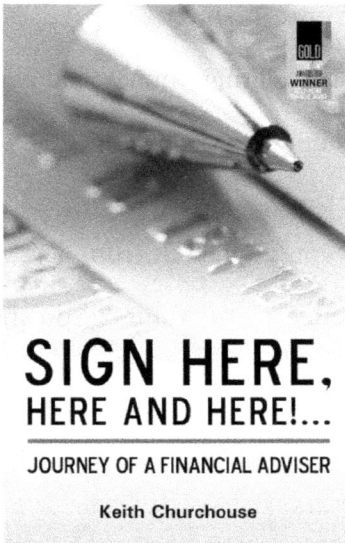

SIGN HERE,
HERE AND HERE!...

JOURNEY OF A FINANCIAL ADVISER

Keith Churchouse

Sign here, here and here! Journey of a financial adviser
The First Churchouse Chronicles
ISBN: 978-0-9564325-0-6

Contents

Foreword

By Sir Christopher Snowden FRS, FREng

As I write this foreword, the global economy is showing signs of recovery from the effects of severe recession. The UK is showing early indications of emergence, with 0.3 per cent growth in the economy in 2012 and encouraging employment statistics in the first months of 2013.

This is the time for companies to seize the opportunities for growth. Economies emerging from recession provide real opportunities for your business and this is the moment to take them. The commercial sector will regain momentum and the business decisions you make in the near future will influence the outcome of your company's success in years to come.

This book is aimed at those who are already running businesses and for aspiring directors, partners and managers of small to medium enterprises (SMEs). It provides thought provoking ideas and challenges for chief executives and leaders of businesses and charities — especially those that appear to have entered a mature phase of development in recent times. This is a book for those who want to evaluate the success of their enterprise and reinvigorate the business and themselves, capturing the author's enthusiasm and experience.

Starting a business can be hard enough, but moving it out of the start-up phase or climbing out of a plateau can be even harder sometimes. Keith Churchouse's book provides informed views, guidance and opinions based on many years' experience in the financial sector. It is aimed at the aspiring businesses that no longer fit into the 'start-up' category, but which have not fully realised their potential or have been focused on surviving the challenges of the recession.

Keith takes a very pragmatic approach in this book, sharing experiences, mistakes and successes. His fresh and energetic style provides the reader with inspiration to make a real difference to the business decisions and directions that are needed in many SMEs to take them on to greater success. The book is aimed at stimulating action by getting managers and business leaders to ask themselves tough questions about planning for the future and assessing where the business is placed today relative to the competition.

I am sure that the highly motivational style of this book will energise your thinking and I hope it contributes to even greater success in your ventures.

Sir Christopher Snowden
March 2013

Sir Christopher Snowden FRS, FREng

Sir Christopher is President and Vice-Chancellor of the University of Surrey and a distinguished engineer with wide experience of the international microwave and semiconductor industry. He has previous experience as a chief executive and as non-executive director of several technology companies and advises several others. He has held research and senior management positions in the electronics industry in both the UK and USA as well as having held academic posts in a number of universities. He is a member of the Prime Minister's advisory Council for Science and Technology and sits on the governing body of the UK's Technology Strategy Board. Sir Christopher is President-Elect of Universities UK, representing all UK universities and Vice-President of the Royal Academy of Engineering. He was President of the Institute of Engineering and Technology 2009-10. He has been a consultant for several major international microwave electronics companies and holds several international awards. Sir Christopher has published eight books and more than 300 technical papers.

Preface

Starting with the end in mind

Most business people start a series of regular processes during their work to reach a successful objective and conclusion. Each business sector is diverse and different and each conclusion and the timing thereof will also vary (however invariably following similar business lines).

The end objective for each business will be different. These commercial plans might change over time to reflect market conditions, competition or overall current business objectives (such as the sale of the company, as an example).

Established and aspiring owner/director managers may choose to re-focus on:

* Production speed
* Production quality
* Sales volumes
* Cash flow, Timing
* Market diversification
* Profitability
* Brand awareness /strength
* All of the above.

The Recession is Over, Time to Grow will encompass many commercial ideas and initiatives and consider the ways that as a maturing SME business, with you as the controller of these issues, might want to focus, re-affirm or re-address each area. You may conclude that you are on course, but many will see that change is needed.

I have read many business books that indicate that they have the solution to all or some of the business issues noted above. Invariably they do not, but they can add value in sharing ideas and opinions in the author's experience. Their business experience and outcomes will be different to others, because each enterprise has its own market challenges.

Why should you read this book if it does not give you all of the answers and solutions to each point? This book, at a critical development phase of our economy, will give you indicators of what others have done and it will give you the valuable opportunity and capacity to take a fresh look at each topic in your own circumstances. I hope my thoughts, observations and notes (along with the notes that you make yourself at the end of each chapter) will be thought provoking and challenging about the processes you use and the key point of *'What is your overall objective?'*

Only you can decide this, but it needs to be clear in your mind what all this hard work that you are putting in is leading to.

These points in turn, with some self-reflection, should allow you to see if your current business path needs to be changed or amended to meet your overall success.

Idea-sized chunks

You are a busy person. You are a business leader and this is what we expect of you.

In seeking to improve your business, and to be ready for growth, there are many ideas within the text of this book, which may take time to absorb and implement. To help you pick out the most relevant points to you and your business,

I have applied sub-headings to each chapter, focussing on individual initiatives and opportunities, idea snap-shots if you like, to help you get the most from your planning and subsequent commercial success.

It really is Time to Grow.

Aide-memoire pages

At the end of each chapter you will find a Note Point where you can detail your own business objectives and ideas, along with key issues in your own business growth strategy.

These notes will be personal to you and your company's needs. You may want to use them to make reference to what your views are currently. They will also act as an aide-memoire for you to revisit, possibly every four to six months or so, to confirm that you remain on course to meet the objectives you have set . . . or make changes if not.

Chapter One: 'Eureka!'

Do you remember that *Eureka!* moment which lifted your very soul? You had that thought: *Let's start a new business!* You can probably remember where you were, what you were doing, the sounds and smells of that marvellous instant.

I was on a train coming back from London to Guildford when it happened to me. My face staring blankly out of a rain-soaked window speeding down the Portsmouth line, I decided that I had to stop my employed drudgery and release my rather smothered potential.

Many people can remember their own *Eureka!* moment, but few of us take the leap of faith and start our own enterprise.

People in their mid-forties have seen recessions before, admittedly in milder form than the recent past. This recent deep recession has proved to be a white-knuckle ride for many of us. With hindsight, perhaps this is not surprising after sixteen years of sustained (and, as it transpires, unsustainable) growth.

For anyone below the age of around thirty-four, this last half-decade of turbulence was their first experience of economic recession — and, more importantly, economic recovery — that they had seen in their working lifetime. It will not be their last.

Which way is the current recession curve now heading? What does it mean for our future economy? The direction and speed of a national or global economy can be likened to a huge cargo ship. It moves slowly. Once momentum is gathered, it's difficult to stop, control or manoeuvre. Direction changes must be planned in advance to achieve any targets. Our economy, along with most westernised systems, has experienced this for many decades as the financial world has evolved, thrived and developed.

This is nothing new. The changes made in the UK by the Bank of England, such as lowering bank base rates (officially known as the Bank Rate) or the use of quantitative easing, take around two years for their full effects to be felt. They have to filter through the economy, targeting specific factors, such as inflation control. It takes calculated decisions to re-ignite an economy, and many global economies are working carefully to achieve this goal.

There are entrepreneurs operating today who have found the tedium of the current economic business climate only just bearable. It would be easy to understand if they feel too weighed down even to notice a positive change, let alone care about it. It will take some conviction for these souls to be persuaded that progress is truly coming. I hope they will read this book and find encouragement in its message.

Taking a step back from your time-pressured daily routine right now is vital.

This is because I believe that the economic curve is changing; it is moving towards a neutral/positive position. You only have to look at global economic factors to see this. Many large companies are finding themselves burdened with massive cash reserves, accumulated during a long-term cautious approach to development. They are now looking for profitable acquisitions into which they can inject this money. Unemployment trends are down and global stock markets, although remaining volatile, are trending upwards.

Business Ambitions — are they still just dreams?

Once started and established, are those business ambitions you once aspired to still your dreams? Or have they become tick-box targets to meet? Do you also remember the motivations that made you take this enormous initial business-creation step? And have these motives come good for you? Be honest now.

For me, I think the answer has to be 'yes' — although had I known the rather relentless nature of running a small business, I think I might not have had so much enthusiasm to get started. I am pleased I did. I had hoped the process of running a business would get easier as the years ticked by. The reality is that the burdens have changed and grown, but so has my ability to deal with the varying issues as they arrive. There are times when a tricky situation or a heavy workload appears, and I can hear myself thinking: *Isn't this similar to last year?* Or, *have we not answered a similar issue before?* Often this is the case and the value of commercial experience starts to show.

Would I do it all again? Without question, the life-learning, challenges and benefits that have enhanced my very being are worth it. Of course there are a few other monetary reasons why it has been worth the toil, energy, and at times exasperations.

However, if I were starting again, I would not start from here! (There will be more on this in a later chapter.) What do I mean by this? Next time I would do it differently, starting with bigger goals and end-targets.

As you will see from this book, there is nothing to stop any SME director from changing his or her model, re-invigorating their proposition and moving up to the next level. We will visit some of these points and initiatives on our journey to greater productivity and profitability.

Headlines sell newspapers

Bad news has always been courted by the press.

Our much criticised and maligned media will always grab the bad news headlines about High Street chains collapsing or business failures, as examples, highlighting difficulties in the retail market's current change process. Sadly, that's what sells papers and news feeds.

Of note globally, there are also headlines being made by Rating Agencies 'downgrading' countries' credit ratings, with many highly-prized AAA ratings being dissolved. I find it interesting that some agencies now administer the downgrade groups of countries *en bloc*, rather than pick out individual victims. Do these downgrades indicate a deterioration in the global economic climate or, partly, a correction of over-optimistic assessments which are now subject to question?

Some experts feel that these past possibly 'generous' ratings of countries, large organisations and securitised debt were part of the cause of the fall into recession from 2007 onwards.

The 'daily dose' of bad news might also make you think that the title of this book is misjudged, showing a lack of empathy for the uphill grind that many SME directors and business owners face every day.

I make no apology for the title. To be clear: the recession *is* over, but I would be the first to agree that we have not seen the positive effects of this change yet.

The reality for all of our business futures is different. Those who pay attention to this economic change opportunity will be the winners at the end of what I predict will be a boom decade.

> *It is not the strongest of the species that survives, nor the most intelligent, but the one most adaptable to change.*
> — Charles Darwin

Others have similar thoughts:

> *You must be the change you wish to see in the world.*
> — Mahatma Gandhi

...*And not a drop to spend!*

I considered calling this book *Business, business everywhere and not a drop to spend!* Have you noticed as a business owner that your company always has far more money than you do personally? Your hard won cash flow is allocated to tax, salaries and marketing budgets. You name it, the cash ebbs and flows here and there and never seems to make it into your own back pocket at the end of the month or trading year.

I was speaking to a very successful director of a medium-sized company which had just expanded into Asia and beyond. His work to make this happen had been masterful. I asked him what his biggest frustration was — and it is just that: significant money around, but by the time it had been wisely managed and allocated, he never seemed to be the real beneficiary. He acknowledged that the business would eventually be sold and cash would be released at that point. But for now, his powerful frustrations remained.

I have felt the same many times. And I am not alone; many director owners claim that some of their staff earned more than they do at times. This is not uncommon during expansion, where the capital burden falls squarely on the business owner.

Company cash flow climbs at certain times in the year (as I note later, you will know when your peak income months are) and it usually draws my attention to the possibility of an extra dividend or bonus that somehow, prudently, evades me. It drives me insane, but keeps both the business in fine financial form and accountants happy.

Forward thinkers

One major key to commercial success is the ability to find quality thinking time. Some forward thinkers block out a point in their diaries to achieve this objective, while others keep a notepad by their bed in which to write down initiatives whilst they remain fresh in their mind.

I communicated by email with a local retailer colleague on this subject, who said: *'I can certainly see the worth in doing something like this and I definitely need some guidance and motivation. To tell you the truth, I am so tired and harassed that I never allow myself time to do anything else [than his day-to-day business]. That includes me and the business.'*

Honest words from a dynamic young man who has everything going for him . . . except time to think.

This is a clear example of the need to slow down and take stock of the situation, in order to speed up into the future.

Business is never so healthy as when, like a chicken, it must do a certain amount of scratching around for what it gets.
— Henry Ford

The industrial revolution . . . online

I believe we are all privileged to have grown up in the current mobile technology era, and to have been able to take on the new computer data techniques and internet opportunities available in the world. Like the industrial revolution a hundred years ago, I do not believe we will see such cultural business change again for another century.

The future years will be dynamic too. The shrinking of the world with globalisation, enabled by the internet, has made more individuals and companies become interactive, enabling them to trade far more easily than before.

I can imagine that when I am a hundred years old (the improvements in medical science are likely to keep me going for this long, although I think I will be even madder by then than I currently am!), I will be watching a documentary on the old invention that is TV on my new computer tablet (version 247), presented by *Sir* Daniel Radcliffe, on how the decades of the 'noughties' and 'teenies' changed our futures forever. The latter part of the documentary chronicling the end of the recession and the return to economic prosperity achieved in this era.

Do not forget that what constitutes *prosperity*, and the way you achieve it, may be different in the future.

The new economic world will be different to the fiscal times we have known in bygone decades. It will not necessarily be better or worse, just different.

A high profile Westminster news reporter, reporting on a recent economic situation while standing late at night in the cold outside the Houses of Parliament, said: *'Teachers change exam questions to get different answers from their students. If an economist sets a question, they keep the question the same; they just expect the answers provided to change.'*

Amusing thoughts. However, the thrust of the message that the future of our economy will be different is correct and will be confirmed by time.

Maybe, when we look back on current times with a futuristic documentary-maker's hindsight, the negative economic effects of this time will be considered first. These might include:

- The collapse of Lehman Brothers Bank
- Falling Bank of England base rates
- Quantitative easing
- The collapse of some big UK based high street retail brands, such as Woolworths and Comet
- Increased direct and indirect taxation (both personal and business)
- Increased business 'Red-Tape' and regulation.

Another key commercial question that has been asked lately challenges one high-profile and previously enduring aspect of our economy: *'Is the High Street dead?'*

The reality is *no*. We are social animals; we enjoy interaction and the hustle and bustle of physical communication in all its forms.

Asking another question may help: *'Is the High Street ready for change in terms of its retail business model?'* This time, the answer has to be *yes*, as it works in some harmony with the internet to attract and retain market share and loyal customers.

I have always maintained that a *customer* only buys once, whereas a *client* returns with regularity.

Brick and click

A new term treading the retail market is *Brick and Click*. Will shops and our High Streets become mere showrooms to browse, rather than to make purchases, with all the buying done over the internet by clicking on your mouse later? In twenty years' time, will our children say they're 'going into town to do some browsing' (rather than shopping)?

You can't smell perfume or after-shave or have a coffee with friends on the internet (yet) and there will always be some need for physical interaction. People also enjoy the personal touch of knowledgeable customer service, which many retailers are good at, even if their business model is outdated and puts them under — or 'only' puts them under threat.

The traditional measure of activity in a High Street store is *foot-fall*: electronic counters measuring physical activity through outlet entrances. Foot-fall may increase in years to come, however *bag-fall* (the number of bags being carried with purchases in them) may reduce as people move to online shopping and delivery to the office or home. The recent expansion of postal services in the UK would further this understanding and, in part, is a welcome boost to our national economy.

Many large retail brands, both in the UK and globally, have reported surges in online sales in recent seasonal peak trading periods, with many parent companies noting lacklustre performances from their High Street outlets. This is a trend also noted in previous years and I am sure it will continue to accelerate. This means that, to survive and prosper, our High Street retailer offerings will have to evolve. So will their competitors. It will be interesting to witness this change process.

What do these comments and observations prove? That there is a dynamic commercial change in the way we undertake shopping in this specific case — but also that the nature of business itself is still evolving.

Within your environment, correctly identifying these trends and embracing the changes is vital to allow your business to make the transition from the pre-recession to the post-recession vibrant, dynamic and, above all, profitable economy.

Indicators from other trading markets

Many other trading markets provide useful information about the future of our national and global economies. Stock markets, commercial property markets and the construction industry all move in different directions, introducing some negative correlation to business productivity and output. These markets provide significant economic indicators about the expectations of the future of our prosperity.

Continued buoyancy in the stock market can indicate a confident approach in future investment prospects. This buoyancy can be fuelled by mergers and acquisitions, both of which show confidence in aligning a business for possible cost-cutting and future growth. It is always interesting to see commercial construction in evidence — a sign of confidence that demand for office or manufacturing or commerce space will be required in the near future.

Have you looked at the plans for the London skyline recently? Building now to meet demand later, it's going against the popular grain of economic pessimism.

Unemployment levels, although remaining at a stubbornly high level, are beginning to fall as employers gear up to boost production again. These indicators point towards sustained future growth and they are all around us. You and I, as leaders of our respective enterprises, need to build on our success to date. We need to be ready and engaged.

Business, more than any other occupation,
is a continual dealing with the future; it is a continual
calculation, an instinctive exercise in foresight.
— Henry R Luce

Your Business Planning

🕐 What is the next 'Big Thing' in your trade/profession/ industry?

🕐 Why this commercial opportunity?

🕐 How will you benefit?

🕐 Why seize this opportunity now?

🕐 What will you have to change?

⏱ How close are you to competing for this new initiative?

⏱ What factors could restrict access to this growth opportunity?

⏱ What do you need to do now to overcome these perceived business growth barriers?

⏱ Who can help you?

⏱ What do you most need now to achieve future success?

The Recession is Over

Chapter Two: Get on with growth

Is the economy, both nationally and internationally, in a better or worse condition than it was before 2007 and the start of the just-ending recession? The answer is neither; it is just *different*.

Will our global economy improve? Yes.

Some countries, such as Brazil, appear to have better prospects than other nations.

Other major nations have grown from being large inward-looking power bases to global economic super-powers over the course of a decade, with the majority of their home markets now enjoying the economic wealth that this brings, as well as the stability of economic maturity.

Many high-end brand exporters are benefiting from this new market prosperity, often while their home markets are still languishing before recovery reaches them. I am sure they will shift back to their natural historic trading zones when this happens. Other countries are seen as fading powers, resigned to their glorious past and still saddled with the debt that came with the glory. Some have referred to this debt mountain as *generational theft*. That's another story.

At the time of writing this book, a referendum on the UK remaining a member of the European Union had been announced and, following the next General Election due in 2015, the great and the good of the UK were expected to have the opportunity to support or leave this economic alliance.

There are many issues to consider in this situation, not least the fact that the UK is a highly vocal participant in the current EU model, without being a full and committed member. If, as a nation, we affirm our acceptance of the EU model then we may have to *really* join, rather than continue to stand on the side-lines as we do today, viewed by some members as the awkward relative.

Could this mean the end of our beloved and valuable currency, Sterling, if we do 'join'? This is a possibility. I think this would be a significant loss, as we move into the future. Those who remember decimalisation in the 1970s may agree. Time and market sentiment for currencies do change. Maintaining a unique currency, in my opinion, gives a nation greater direct control of its fiscal affairs.

Help for start-ups . . . then over to you

The amount of help available to generate new business start-ups is significant. From free training to so-called 'free' banking facilities, amongst others, the enthusiastic offers to start-ups are all encouraging. They are certainly welcome at the outset.

We all know that there is no such thing as a free lunch. I have no doubt that these offers are a profitable way of gaining good future income by providing introductory give-aways to start-ups that will eventually reach maturity and profitability.

What is missing, as you may have noticed, is any significant help for those companies that have already survived the incubator phase, have grown to some maturity, and then want to grow thereafter. Those companies, such as yours and mine, need to move to the next level of business generation, creating further jobs, corporate innovation and tax revenues.

There is also significant financial support for large, usually multi-national companies to relocate to areas or countries, with on-going financial support seemingly easy to find.

I find this lack of interest in the mid-group SME area both strange and somewhat incomprehensible, because this is exactly what our national economy needs: growing and thriving established SMEs. You will not get tomorrow's UK-based large companies without pushing established SMEs on further.

As business leaders, if we are alone then we only have each other to rely on, to share business wisdom and acumen, and to help in our quest for additional success. This is where some focused networking and collaboration is worthwhile, as you will see in Chapter Nine.

Sharing enterprise learning from my own business growth will, I hope, provide you with insight into what you need to be planning now. Many industries and professions, along with government bodies, recommend and facilitate this sharing with the aim of moving enterprise forward at a faster and more productive rate.

> *Education is the most powerful weapon which you can use to change the world.*
> — Nelson Mandela

Board meetings or bored meetings?

Most well-run businesses have Board minutes from previous trading periods, noting key business decisions and issues that were affecting the business at the time they were made.

Let us be careful to note that, for an SME, a Board meeting does not have to mean sitting at a large table with a group of executives nodding or objecting to ideas and decisions. A Board meeting can be you and fellow directors or advisers considering the same things over a glass of wine at the end of the day. As long as the meeting and the agreed outcomes are formally documented, this should suffice.

Our most recent 'Board meeting' was over breakfast with our accountant. It was an inspiring gathering with lots of ideas and motions agreed, including the implementation of time frames. The coffee was strong and so were the innovations being discussed.

It is great to stand back from the day-to-day issues, preferably on neutral ground without emails distracting you, to look at what is really happening and what could be achieved more efficiently. If a Board meeting becomes a 'bored' meeting, you have to figure out what is going wrong.

Board minutes are an easy reference point to use for planning and progression. They should remind, re-inspire and direct you to the next phase. Minutes also convert well to serve as an agenda in discussing with your other stakeholders, such as your staff and even your bank, some of the ideas, difficult decisions, and objectives of the business.

It is also a great challenge to see what was planned previously and what the outcomes were. If all agreed points were not implemented, why not?

Should they be actioned now? Only if you want to move forward.

No more 'boom and bust'? Rubbish!

You cannot have an economic bust without a boom. And neither can you have a boom without a bust, irrespective of what any past Chancellor of the Exchequer would have you believe.

The flow of an economy is like carrying water in a bucket, sloshing about as it moves: you know that the more it tilts one way, the more it goes the other way on its return. This is the way of a capitalist economy and commerce.

As an experiment, if you gave a hundred people £100 each and asked them to trade with each other over a day, you would have some with no money by the end of the day and others with lots. That is the way of free trade.

Knowing this, what can you do to make profit and value by both enhancing the swell of your own business and, more importantly, riding the crests of the new business waves as they come through?

Why more businesses fail on the way out of recession

It is well known that smaller companies can be nimble on their feet when it comes to commerce, procurement, proposition and profitability. Any business leader knows that *profit* is not a dirty word. These are some of the advantages of being an SME, leading to the notion that *small is beautiful.*

Both 'small' and 'beautiful' are words open to definition and you can decide what they both mean to you and your enterprise.

Maybe it would be better to say *'lean is beautiful',* as an alternative to small. In business, this is usually true.

Larger companies, usually nationals, are often more cumbersome in their ability to make quick market moves, a bit like the cargo ship we noted in Chapter One, they can move too slowly. They fill the headlines at certain times of the year (deep winter being a favourite) with some apparently strong brands going to the wall.

In a recent round of these headline-grabbers, many people argued that they were surprised that the organisations in question had survived so long, citing outdated trading models or, alternatively, updated trading models that had not gone far enough in their transition to new markets, delivery propositions and environments. One example is the transition to internet downloads from CD sales, which has negated in part the need for High Street stores, offering the physical (in this case CD's) items.

It is of note that there are now retail outlets where you can order online and collect in-store, that seem to be bucking the trend and even setting a new profit line.

Could these failing enterprises be accused of arrogance, lack of vision, over-promising and under-delivering, indecision, inability to grasp new concepts and ideas that reflect a changing business environment? Probably some or all of the above.

Staying the same as you were, going into a recession, is usually not a viable strategy when coming out of recession. Markets, products, clients and buying processes evolve and so should your business. The new post-recession trading world will have changed and you know that your business should evolve to maximise the emerging advantages.

Is it failure or is it accounting?

Business failures are not uncommon. It is interesting to read behind the headlines to see if the collapse of an organisation is a real *failure*, or whether it can be seen more as a proficient accounting measure. I have recently seen the latter being referred to as 'pre-pack' administration, where a phoenix organisation rises from the ashes in a pre-arranged deal.

I have met some 'distress CEOs' who are parachuted into organisations by their owners or by the appointed administrators with the objective of finding and communicating three options:

1.   The business is viable, with appropriate changes/ re-focus/ re-marketing;

2.   The assets are viable, and so are parts of the business; other parts (possibly including some staff sectors/ branch locations) are not financially viable. This may involve a degree of asset-stripping to create value for the owners/ administrators;

3.   The business is not salvageable.

There is no wrong or right answer in the investigative exercise above. Little emotion is applied, just a clinical decision-based process on the framework and facts that surround the ailing organisation. These are usually the extreme options of last resort. This could indicate a business that has lost its way, a situation *you* will not allow to arise by planning and implementing your commercial objectives carefully.

Business and the UK are not alone in thinking about the way organisations are managed into the future.

> Referring to his own Government and its aspirations, Barack Obama noted:
> *It's time to fundamentally change the way we do business in Washington. To help build a new foundation for the twenty-first century, we need to reform our Government so that it is more efficient, more transparent, and more creative. That will demand new thinking and a new sense of responsibility for every dollar that is spent.*

Breaking the (perceived) production ceiling

In my own situation, the first few years of our business went well. Energy levels remained high and the lust to produce sales and service was at the front of both the team's and my mind. Being passionate and focused about what you do makes this a lot easier. Attitude and belief in what you are doing can be everything in making your objectives happen.

There are many examples of entrepreneurs who have maintained both of these attributes in getting their product off the ground in the face of adversity. A few such products are now household names. Each of them received many product perfection challenges, and sometimes rejections, before they found their place in the market . . . and ultimately their success. Examples you might want to consider are Colonel Sanders, Thomas Edison, Norm Larsen and his water displacing spray, along with many others.

Clearly, in these examples, ambition and determination to succeed shone through. To break through any production ceiling that you face, you will need to have ambition, determination, attitude and belief . . . lots of it.

First plateau

We celebrated our first six-month business period to the end of our accounting trading year end, and achieved sales proved that there might after all have been some method in our commercial madness.

The first full year saw the production accelerator being pushed to the floor; the second full trading year saw the sales pedal being pushed through the floor and out the other side. We really were motoring. Then, into the third year, we saw a rather frustrating production 'levelling', which continued into years four and five. We had hit a ceiling, or plateau, which seemed unbreakable.

In reaching our first production plateau, in the fourth and fifth years, my frustration was obvious. Everything seemed contrary to the preceding years where we had achieved significant growth of approximately 100 per cent each year. This initial achievement had been created from a fresh field, but became unsustainable thereafter, only seeing thirty per cent growth in the third full year and approximately seven per cent in the fourth full year.

The production graph from our start to this point looked like a wilting daffodil, flattening in the middle.

If ever there was a moment to say *something needs to change*, then this was it. The accounts for the previous years had shown, within a tolerance of five per cent or so, the same final figures (after increasing costs).

I once had an employment income like this, where I received three years of P60 tax documents showing similar salary incomes. With annual inflation at five per cent at the time, my real income was going noticeably backwards. I could not influence the situation at work, so I influenced the issue the only way I could, by getting another job.

It would have been easier to have accepted the situation and to carry on. But good business people do not accept second best; that's why you are reading this book.

Growth at any cost?

What is an appropriate level of growth that a SME business owner should consider when forward planning?

A business colleague of mine, Rebecca, who owns a maturing business, suggests that 100 per cent growth in both turnover and profit as a minimum over two years should be 'easily' achievable. If she doesn't do it, she believes she will have 'failed'. Having aggressive targets is admirable; as long as you have the initial team 'buy-in', infrastructure, and cash flow to feed the process, then these high targets may well be viable.

Against the backdrop of a weak and recovering national economy, some might fairly argue that this targeting level is folly, and only serves to demonstrate arrogance. I would disagree in part. As long as the proposed target is well thought through, the relevant journey indicators mapped and the process challenged on a regular basis, high production growth rates should be attainable — and, more importantly, sustainable.

Arrogance can be a good business tool, if it is not over used. So can an eye for detail, and this will be required to attain the planned high growth requirements above.

Cutting off your troops

There are many examples of businesses that expand rapidly and then, on faltering, contract at the same speed, with many casualties. Too many warzone battles have shown similar strategy examples in misguided invasions, only for supply lines to be disrupted and troops cut off. The real casualties of war are a greater human cost than the fiscal casualties of a business. Do not let this happen when delivering *your* business expansion strategy.

> *Ten soldiers wisely led will beat a hundred without a head.*
> — Euripides

Are you a morning or an afternoon person?

I am not going to dwell on this subject for long, because there are plenty of time management books that can detail the benefits of various systems and theories. The two significant points I would raise are simple. The first one is: *Are you a morning or an afternoon person*?

The second point is: *Knowing which you are, do you make the most of the opportunity this presents?*

I am a morning person, hungry to do the day's work, writing and planning in the early to mid-morning period, tailing off in the afternoon. I always wake with the aim that I am going to learn something new today. However small or large the point is, it is new. A lust to learn is never a bad thing. Some might argue that I am useless in the evening, but that's another story.

Others do not wake their business brains until after lunch and then move up to top gear in the late afternoon and early evening. Each to their own. Recognising which time zone in a working day suits your best productivity (and that of your key employees) and planning your day around your peak creative performance times is imperative to get the best from your most important assets, namely you and your energy.

Plan your day around your energy levels

You might want to reconsider this energy issue and plan key meetings, seminars and presentations around the periods that engage the best performance times for you. The Notes section on the next page may help focus your aspirations and targets.

Your Business Planning

🕐 What are the business decisions you regret and admire? Why?

_____

_____

_____

_____

🕐 Have you evolved your business model since the recession began? How?

_____

_____

_____

_____

🕐 Is your business proposition and model ready for increased business productivity?

_____

_____

_____

_____

🕐 How can you enhance this preparation now? What will you do?

_____

_____

_____

_____

⏱ Are your increased production plans realistic and mapped for your team to understand and follow?

⏱ What single additional point could you undertake now, a possible 'curve-ball', to lift your plans by five per cent? Challenge your plan to squeeze one more advantage out.

⏱ When is your most productive time of the day and could you use this advantage?

⏱ Could you change your weekly diary to this timing/ productivity advantage?

Chapter Three: Are you the person for the job?

We have all personally changed since starting the new businesses we have successfully nurtured over the last few years. It would be impossible not to. In general, I think the process makes individuals harder, more direct, focussed and more determined as time has moved on. With the volume of routine business decision making needed, it is unsurprising that a successful individual naturally becomes more decisive.

Bearing in mind that your full time occupation — running the company show — may be your speciality, are you the right person for the job in bringing new change for your company to a profitable conclusion? Could someone who has precisely this expertise do this for you in a more cost effective and timely fashion?

Now might be the time for you to concentrate on what you excel at, and allow a specialist or aspiring team leader to lead the next challenge of taking the business to the next level.

A steady hand

You may have been quite the maverick when you first started the business, breaking free from the chains of employment to make the business the success it is today. The recession may have knocked off some of those dynamic edges to turn you into a mature executive decision maker. Now your role is making sure that the ship that is your business keeps its sails trimmed and its course out of choppy waters.

You may have been unaware of this process of personal change, and find yourself needing to restore the old maverick passion that got you going in the first place. You will need to re-find this for the next push to business success.

> *Whenever an individual or a business decides that success has been attained, progress stops.*
> — Thomas J Watson

Store of cash

Ironically, you could find that becoming a safe pair of hands has meant that, rather than investing in the infrastructure of the company, you have stored cash as reserves. Possibly increasing the comfort zone that you may have slipped into? A cash reserve, although usually prudent business planning, may make your company attractive to an acquirer in its own right. Someone could buy your company for cash and then, once the purchase is complete, simply extract the cash they have just purchased. They may then use the other assets for their own business or sell these on. This is not an unknown practice, sometimes referred to as *asset stripping*.

Ready and willing to...

As a business owner/director, you invariably also became the chief cook and bottle washer, undertaking all tasks, intellectual and manual, to get the project at hand going. The passion you have for your product/service will drive this.

You will have shone at various tasks and may not be so strong in other areas. Are you ready and willing (and most importantly able) to:

- Increase sales of the current model offerings through current outlets?
- Develop new outlets for greater distribution and market share?
- Generate a completely new distribution model?
- Diversify your business to attract a new untapped market?
- Reduce or increase prices by making changes to your product or service to attract a different buying demographic?
- Compete against yourself (and more importantly your competition) by introducing a new brand line or outlet? As examples, this has proved successful in the household detergent market, and also for some retail shops also having an online channel.
- Expand into yet unchartered waters for your business, such as international markets? There are underdeveloped hemispheres that could greatly use your expertise.
- A different and improved marketing approach to your existing proposition?
- Some or all of the above?

These are only examples of what could and should be considered and you will have other additions to this proactive list.

I have expanded on some of the points you may want to consider in this economic transition phase below.

Distribution increase

You may have noted by now that I have written a few books. These are based in the UK market, which in itself has some limitations, especially for those who do not read English.

I attended a seminar given by an eminent global economist who talked about the significant opportunities offered by the developing regions of Brazil, Russia, India and China. As a UK-based SME owner, I was excited by the information — and at the same time felt that there was little realistic opportunity for my businesses to be involved in this global growth. I was perplexed by this challenge and the feeling stayed with me for some time.

I realised that if we were able to have my existing books translated into Portuguese (for the Brazilian market), we could increase distribution significantly and the opportunity to make greater success from the existing publications. After investigation, we already had (but had not identified that) the systems in place to release the books in Brazil, along with other Portuguese speaking nations. Bearing in mind that the population of Brazil is about three times the size of the UK (excluding the greater Global potential), this increases the potential for sales and distribution significantly. Brazil was identified because it has the potential and is hungry to develop, evolve and thrive.

A great opportunity was seized and achieved. The additional production costs were not high, the process (once a suitable translator based in Rio was sourced) was not challenging and the outcome has taken the business books to a global level.

Thinking outside the box in this case was worthwhile. Thinking this through a stage further, and using this example, what could *your* company change (either in its product/service or distribution) to increase the opportunities to grow, hopefully at low cost, introducing an economy of scope? (There will be more about this excellent commercial concept later.)

To develop your business into the future, you now have to decide in which ways you will make changes. If you need to make changes in more than one way — and be careful about spreading resources too thinly, if you do — you will need to prioritise these plans.

This leads to the question as suggested by the chapter title: *Are you the person for the job?*

It is reported that Abraham Lincoln said:
If there is anything that a man can do well, I say let him do it. Give him a chance.

New Year's resolution

One business owner I met had set himself a New Year's resolution on the subject of making changes to what he gave to the business. The belief that we are coming out of recession and that this needs to be planned for is shared by many people. His resolution for the forthcoming year was simple: *'To change my job!'* Not in the literal sense of leaving to find other employment, but to stop what he was doing, the day-to-day running of the company, and to re-focus on what he *should* be doing, which in this case was winning new business.

His main resolution was to incorporate a new senior member to his team to allow his thriving business momentum to continue.

I asked him why the transformation now? He explained that the company was reaching some maturity and with this they were winning bigger contracts because, he felt, of the continued energy and drive of the company and its stability. On winning bigger contracts, they were then winning additional contracts of similar if not larger value. They say success breeds success and this may be proof.

Jack of all trades

You can see that we have already covered a kaleidoscope of business specialities, and will consider further the change challenges you should consider such as marketing, PR, human resources, research and development, product redesign and unit cost re-pricing.

You should never be a 'Jack of all trades and master of none', especially in commerce. Trying to be all things to all men never works effectively. Take a careful look at the aspects of any new objectives set and make sure that these are delegated to the people with the best aptitude for those segments of the overall task.

In doing this, you may find that you do not have the right person within your team to nail a specific objective or function. Outsourcing to a specialist, whether it be an individual or a company, who can work with the team for this specific task may well be the best and most cost effective solution. You may be able to import these required services.

This is something we have undertaken in the past for specific specialist issues, and we continue to do so, with cost effective results. External input also provides interesting intelligence that can give your own organisation greater depth. You can always learn from others.

> *Tell me and I forget, teach me and I remember,*
> *involve me and I learn.*
> — Benjamin Franklin

Stop for a moment to think about whether you should also export some of the services you provide as an opportunity.

Research and development

Many countries realise that the real value within their economy is in *intellectual property*. You may still be able to get tax relief and grants for R&D (Research and Development) work within your business, subject to various criteria. You might want to investigate this and its terms before starting a project to see if additional funding can be gained. If you can source a grant, this could provide a valuable cash flow tool and possibly reduce the impact of a new front-loaded, high-development cost project.

Economies of scope

I am a great fan of the theories of 'economies of scope'. This is different from 'economies of scale', which means reducing average unit cost.

Economies of scope refers to lowering average cost for a company in producing two or more products from the same item, diversifying its application. Effectively, more people can be reached per monetary unit spent. You may want to look at this study further; the concept and term were created by Panzar and Willig (1977, 1981), in their work 'Economies of Scale in Multi-Output Production'.

Economies of scope is a way that your product or offering can be applied to other applications. For example, the basic body floor plan for one car model is used by one master group on many of its various individual brand lines, expanding the range of the use of the design into new markets and reaching more people. The final models look very different, are marketed differently, but use the same components underneath.

Negotiate fixed costs hard at the outset . . . and at renewal stage

One major issue when reducing costs is your own negotiating skills. These will have been honed over the years you have been running your own company and using the company's money. There are many ways to control price-based negotiation situations, such as *anchoring* or, to a lesser extent, *framing*.

*Anchoring (*or *Focalism* as it is sometimes referred to)* follows a different psychology from price negotiation and runs against the normal process of rounded price points — but may well save you money. Normally we, and our contacts and consumers, follow 'herd' mentality by expecting prices and counter-offers to be *rounded* (such as £70,000, as an example) — even though we know there is no rational reason why they should be. This points to the human tendency to rely too heavily on the first piece of information, in this case price, offered. The opportunity to apply some different logic in the form of *anchoring* (which might produce a price of £67,137) can, if used wisely, be an effective business tool when negotiating. This process was first theorised by Kahneman and Tversky.

Price *Framing* is another well studied tactic and marketing tool. When you consider the price of a product or service, someone has decided its value when bringing it to market.

Why does a family car typically cost around £20,000? That's not what it costs to produce. The product price has been presented or *framed* to the end user, which may influence their decision making process. A price frame can be a reflection of competitor pricing, or simply a starting point for negotiation. The Office of Fair Trading (OFT) produced a paper on this subject, *The impact of price frames on consumer decision making* through their Chief Economist, Dr Amelia Fletcher in 2010.

Each method, and there are many others, has its attributes. It is worth getting to know these in order to hone your own negotiations and the control of future business budgets.

Cost control and other unforeseen benefits

In one of my previous books, *Sign here, here & here!*, I observed that we relocated our company premises around the corner to a High Street address after approximately two years of trading.

The reasons for the move (more space, the risk of the first building being re-developed which it subsequently was, and a general need to grow) were varied, but not directly profit related. They had more to do with affordability, which can be just as important.

We negotiated hard on the lease cost and term — and for our future prosperity we needed to. I meet too many business owners who have a great business model, but did not pay full attention or negotiate hard enough at the point of signing on the dotted line for their premises lease. Saddled with high 'negotiated' rents and a long lease without a break clause, they will always have an uphill battle towards profitability, sustainability and success.

The net effect of our own move, and admittedly a little extra marketing, were as follows:

- We immediately put our prices up
- The number of enquiries went up
- The *quality* of enquiries jumped dramatically
- Profitability went up
- Old enquirers came back with renewed confidence
- The gestation period from sale to payment lengthened to six weeks from three to four weeks (which was a critical cash flow point and one to keep a keen eye on).

Anyone wishing to be critical of my experience could easily argue that these points should have been the reasons for making the move in the first place; they would be right. I hope that my own lessons will help you avoid any pitfalls in your own business plans and their location.

Do consider the positives and negatives of a relocation move. Location and access can be the most important issues for your customers and clients, irrespective of the type of business you run. If in doubt, ask them!

Cojones!

Life and success, in the modern world, is a construction partly based on who has the biggest '*Cojones*' from cradle to grave. (In case you don't know, the English term for '*Cojones*' is rather crude and refers to a part of a gentleman's anatomy, symbolising his masculinity.)

From the playground onwards, he who hits the hardest rules the playground. In business, it is sometimes a matter of whoever is prepared to take the biggest commercial risks, either on a single occasion or on a regular basis, achieves significant success.

It's almost like a game of Dare: taking ever-bigger risks in the hope that something won't break. For the risk-taker, this attitude, possibly rhetoric-based and bravado-led, will continue into retirement, as they pass on these skills and wisdom to the younger generation.

You can see this in all walks of life. Invariably, the CEO of a company, or a senior Partner, did not get where he or she is by being kind and accommodating to everyone along the way. The athletes perennially training on the playing fields are usually only there because they are prepared to do the most to succeed. The best divorce lawyer is usually the most ruthless.

When is the last time you took a calculated business risk?

By taking the jump to business owner (from wherever you were before), you are by definition already a risk taker. Congratulations, however be mindful of this when planning ahead. It can make you a hard person to deal with if not controlled occasionally.

> *I suppose leadership at one time meant muscles; but today it means getting along with people.*
> — Mahatma Gandhi

No hurry . . . in some situations

When we started our company, a previous employer instructed solicitors to contact us, demanding that we stop trading within

48 hours in the belief that we were marketing to their client base. This was not the case but the letter clearly was no joke. I was not sure whether to laugh or to be concerned. Guessing was not the best option in this situation and we promptly sought a referral to a local solicitor as a precautionary measure.

As a budding but relatively green entrepreneur, I was shocked by this ex-employer affront. I certainly had not anticipated this approach, let alone within the first month of trading. My business *'Cojones'* were not, shall we say, fully developed. If intimidation had been the objective, then it had achieved its goal.

After taking some legal advice, our newly acquired solicitor prepared and applied a robust response, with similar bravado, suggesting that, if they wished to pursue their allegations of competition, we would be more than pleased to entertain a legal action.

However, our response was deliberately delayed by our legal counsel to ensure that we defied both their approach and the time frame they had specified.

This tactic chimed with the thinking of a senior solicitor client I knew well, who also suggested: *'Leave it in the top drawer for a few days before you do anything with it.'* This proved to be the prudent thing to do and, after an acknowledgement of our response, we did not hear further from our opponents.

This situation was also a good example of an unforeseen business set-up expense. Our contingency fund was wiped out by the legal expenses and we managed to maintain our cash flow position — only just — by planning to build up a contingency fund.

Sleep on it

Personally, I have never been one to 'sleep on it'. As a director, I believe it is good to be decisive and to take firm action, reacting to everything that crosses your desk or computer screen. Some may assume that such swift responses are due to you not having thought about the answer; they do not understand that it is a talent that has been honed by your business experience. This is precisely why you are who you are, in the position you maintain.

However, as my wisdom has grown (and other situations including legal business positions have come along) taking a little time to think about the way you want to go forward has often been the wise choice. It is too easy to react to an issue and later feel that you might have reacted more constructively if you had slept on it first.

First draft

I now often find myself drafting a response to a situation and then leaving it overnight.

An employer I once worked for suggested that your 'gut feel' is the right one, and on many occasions she was right. Leaving some prepared thoughts to stew overnight allows for reflection and consideration.

Amendments can be applied in the morning and then, if significant, left again for a further night before being submitted.

I find this a challenging way of dealing with a situation, especially when I feel perfectly able to make quick decisions and to respond accordingly, usually on a high volume basis, every day. However, the maturity you harvest from your business activities can show prowess in these situations. Almost invariably, there is no real need to hurry at such times; taking a step back and dwelling on the situation before providing a response can save money and time.

This is not always the case, though. Building a team of focused reliable professional contacts, such as a good solicitor and accountant, will pay you dividends on those other occasions when your own thinking is not enough.

Your Business Planning

🕐 Looking at your business product/service: could it be applied to a new market to increase market share? How?

🕐 Is the cost of this change affordable and achievable? Why/ why not?

🕐 What are you best at in the business? Why?

🕐 Is the work you apply yourself to the right type?

🕐 Are the tasks you undertake using the real value you could bring to the business? What changes will you introduce?

🕐 Could anyone else reduce your workload to allow you thinking and development time?

🕐 Have you reviewed your fixed costs? When/How?

When are these contracts (and associated costs) to be renewed? Have you considered alternatives?

🕐 Could you reduce business acquisition costs and increase profit by outsourcing?

🕐 Similarly, could you profitably export more of your services/knowledge/product to other companies?

🕐 Are you ready for challenges to your business model?

Chapter Four: Wonky wheel

I have often heard that you need to get your work/life balance correct. After two divorces, it might fairly be suggested that I am not that good at this balance. I think this is because I have a passion for my business and I make no apology for that. I love what I do and this makes the whole process of work a lot easier.

The commercial demands for a successful SME are usually high and many owner/director/partners will know that taking your eye off the ball can lead to some 'wonky wheels' falling off the business wagon — or indeed disrupting your home life. You can usually only have two proverbial horses in a race, but only one will win!

The passion for your company and its offering should extend to all areas of your business and every client contact.

Your success will rely on your quality communications and the trust of you and your brand.

Trust

Trust is an amazing thing; not easily created and so easily lost. You cannot see it, box it or touch it, but you know it exists.

I recently attended a presentation that suggested, '*Trust is the currency of persuasion*'.

That thought is relevant to all business relationships, from staff, to co-directors, to your clients.

The same presentation was littered with under-used words, probably to stimulate interest. Normally we are encouraged in business to use straight, clear language — but clearly on this occasion I took something from it.

One word, *reciprocity*, used during this seminar was relevant to the issue of trust, where give-and-take (rather than financial profit/loss) helps to generate an environment of trust and rapport between participants. *Reciprocity* is something we all use, not always consciously. It means knowing who and why we trust other people. Some might say this is the difference between emotional profit and loss. It made me think about people with whom I had *reciprocity*. The list was sadly short but nonetheless, of great value to me and I hope to those I share this trust with.

Stand back and keep sane

It is easy to be consumed by your business. You live and breathe it every day. I have been accused in the past of being *intense*, so it is rather ironic that with some directorship experience now secured on my CV, I suggest that you *do not* take yourself too seriously.

Moving out of recession and being reminded of the potential administrative drudgery of recent years can weigh you down, whether you realise it or not. Regulation and red tape do not go away. Maybe the saying about the certainties of life should be extended to include death, taxes *and regulation*.

These thoughts should also remind you of your business strengths and areas for development of what you do best.

Are you a hunter or a farmer?

Are the values, both personal and business, that you held all that time ago when you started the business, the same as you have now? Many good business plans are born out of adversity, especially following this lengthy recessionary period.

In my case, I had just finished a divorce and thought that I could offer a better and more personalised service proposition. My previous employment was not going in the direction I had expected and a change was needed, as confirmed by that 'Eureka' moment noted in Chapter One.

Starting a new business with nothing is daunting. I have already suggested in this text that it was the biggest (and, as it turns out, the best) step I have ever taken in my working life. It certainly brings out the business *hunter* in you.

Now that the business is up and running, some security has been established, and *farming* the business has increased in priority, instead of only winning new business (or *hunting*).

Were you a business hunter or a business farmer when you started the enterprise? Which are you now? What inspired you to start? Is the work you do now still inspiring you?

There are many good business books that suggest that if you are not growing production (in whatever that production occurs in your business, such as sales, services sold, commodity sales), you are effectively going backwards. If you build inflationary pressures into this equation, then it's true. You may need to go 'hunting' again.

Looking forward, what do you want to be, a *hunter* or *farmer*? What does the business need? The two answers could well be different and it is important to review this now.

Hunter turned farmer?

I like hunting. The thrill of winning new business still gives me the buzz that I thrive on. However, after eight years of production, I also have a lot of existing clients and assets to care for that need, to use the term, *farming*. We have a gap in our production model and a solution to it.

We have introduced a new member of staff to cater for this identified situation, which will help our business grow by securing the assets we already hold. The identified development need was not itself a problem, but it could have been if it had not been addressed. This business change also frees my time to do what I do best: win new business.

These changes are only a reaction to the changing need of the business as it grows. This can only be good, and this sense of positive evolution should be embraced. It can be all too easy for a business leader to stick his or her head in the sand and expect the growth pains to disappear. The important point is identifying the growth need and, of course, addressing it when suitable volume creates a profitable opportunity.

It is all part of the process of preparing and being ready for the upturn that is on the horizon. And it matters now, whether or not you can actually see that upturn in the distance.

Taking the time to care for your business needs is vital. Sometimes, going back to your original core values and basics of your initial plans is what is needed.

If you do not look back to go forward, you could be very busy, but for all the wrong reasons.

Busy people

If you want to get something done, ask a busy person. However, be careful of the busy fools who seem to be ever so busy, but do not achieve much more than a lot of 'huff and puff'.

When our business runs at over fifty per cent capacity, which is usual, the business processing takes on a flow of its own, creating efficiencies in performance. Accuracy also remains high.

On a few occasions in the calendar year (deep summer being a good example; people tend to feel hot and lethargic), we find that production falls below fifty per cent of capacity. It is at these times that I find motivation sometimes wanes in the team. Accuracy is always maintained, but only with the introduction of extra checks to ensure that full attention has been applied. Whether this situation affects your existing business lines or new business ideas, be ready to use this potential gift of identified time valuably.

> *Until you value yourself, you won't value your time.*
> *Until you value your time, you will not do anything*
> *with it.*
> — M Scott Peck

New projects just need (down) time

How many times in a year do you stumble across a new and beneficial business idea? Many I hope, each one being real opportunity.

Whether it is suggested by one of the team or has just sprung into your mind, all this opportunity needs is a little thinking time and application, both of which are in short supply when your machine is running at full speed. This is an inconvenient truth of business.

Keeping a note of these ideas in busy times, and implementing them in low production periods, is productive and can be, as I have found, inspirational to team members who may otherwise be less focused (in the summer in our earlier example). If you map your last five years' production on a graph month by month, you will see the trends and identify the quieter times when new project implementation can be instigated, without damaging other outputs.

For me, 'quieter time' is usually when I'm on holiday, when my brain gears down a little, but still ticks over with *'what if we...'* ideas, confirming the points we have reached, and the progress yet to be made. I always make notes of these new initiatives and achievable ideas and bring them back to the office on my return.

Whatever you do, it is important to consider how these ideas can be applied and possibly, more importantly, when you can apply them to maximum effect.

Economies of scope (again) for the sale of business assets

You may have strived hard on building your brand and product, hopefully successfully. Like me, you may have enjoyed this challenge.

Questions for you to consider:

- Why did you build just one brand product?
- If you were building one anyway, why didn't you build two or three alternatives at the same time?
- If, like me, you didn't, why not do it now?

The potential benefit of this planning is that you might be able to sell each brand separately, or as a group with or without the main company. Selling product lines or brands separately may give you greater flexibility and the opportunity to bring sale funds into the main business, without selling the main company.

Competing to increase market share through creating additional brands has long been proved to be successful, if it is carefully planned. You have to carefully focus so that you do not overly detract from your own main product, but may be able to gather additional profitable income from other markets. Many large corporates undertake this strategy: buying up smaller profitable brands along the way if they start to eat into their own market share. Competition from others may not be a bad situation and may lift the overall level of demand for your product/service within a market sector.

I am sure you would not object to a large corporation making you a *profitable* offer to take your product off your hands.

To achieve this you are likely to need the 'buy-in' from your team. Keeping them motivated is vital.

Changing the workplace environment

Is making workplace environment changes something you could or should consider?

You may have never considered these issues since you opened your doors all those years ago. It is very easy for both you and your team to get into a groove (or rut in some cases!) as time ticks by. Does the adage *a change is as good as a rest* apply?

We have to balance this comment by adding the one about *do not fix what is not broken*. However, maybe a change around in your physical business environment would be worthwhile, even if that only amounts to a redecoration, which may also be long overdue.

You do not want your employees getting bored and under-motivated in a lacklustre work environment. Many organisations operate a rotation system of their staff every two or three years to help them develop and to give them greater interaction with their co-workers and the overall business objective. This usually also provides a greater depth of commercial understanding, keeps desks tidy because they are not going to be there indefinitely, and it keeps the team on their toes.

With the latest and ever-evolving business communication facilities now available, and while you are thinking outside the box, do you still need an office or premises at all? Maybe you do, but I wanted to encourage you to think about alternatives.

Are the reasons why you located to the premises you have now still relevant? As your business model continues to develop, does your location (or facility type, office to warehouse or other premises) need to change and develop?

Experiments from history

You may think that changing the workplace environment — this includes both positive and negative changes — may not improve production. However, experiments from the past suggest otherwise.

Some of the earliest and most famous of these were the Hawthorne experiments of Elton Mayo. Mayo was a Harvard professor who conducted these experiments between 1927 and 1932 in Chicago, around the time of the Great Depression. The studies grew out of preliminary experiments at the Western Electric Hawthorne Works, from 1924 to 1927, on the effect of light on productivity. It was a great study and well worth a read if you get a chance, with Elton spending his last days in Surrey, England.

The summary of these experiments suggested, among other things, that it did not matter what the employer did (both positive changes and retraction of the original changes), including the removal of all the improvements. The consequence was that output production went up or, at worst, stayed the same.

What are the findings of the study? It appears that the attention and freedom given to the workers (in this instance) created better teamwork and co-operation.

Could you apply this type of approach to your team to improve production and possibly innovation?

> Alan Greenspan, retired chairman of the US Federal Reserve, noted that:
> *I have found no greater satisfaction than achieving success through honest dealing and strict adherence to the view that, for you to gain, those you deal with should gain as well.*

You want the best from and for your team and your company. As an observation, it never fails to astound me how some company owners pay attention to the environment of their offices or factory , but then don't clean the entrance sign welcoming all-comers. To me, this says: *'We are here, although we're not that interested in you.'* When you speak to the owner you know this is not the case. I only tell them once about their sign and the blinkers come off . . . as does the grime from their Welcome company sign. First impressions really do count.

Taking the blinkers off to take a fresh look at what you have created is both rewarding and necessary to enjoy the rest of the journey to prosperity. Take a walk around your company today and see what's good . . . and what's not!

It is important to take pride in the community you work in and the way you represent and present your company.

Give something back . . .

Assuming you have been successful and built a great business, then the likelihood is that you did not do it alone. You will have had a team around you (at home, you probably have a family team who support you as well), probably small at the outset and grown thereafter. I have added good reminders in this chapter that these teams need looking after, both in terms of their working environments and their overall peace of mind.

I would also add that the community that provides you with business also needs some reciprocal help and guidance. This *community* can be your trade area, other businesses, professional body, forums or even simply the public in your location. Some would take this further by suggesting that, as a business leader, it is your responsibility, or even your *obligation* to do so. You may not have had a Corporate Social Responsibility (CSR) strategy when you first started your business, simply because that was unaffordable at the time — but you should probably consider one now.

No one has ever become poor by giving.
— Anne Frank

It is likely that, like me, you are bombarded with requests to offer varied support every week, if not daily. It is worth taking time, either directly or through one of your team, to look at whom and what you could support — but do keep it down to only one or two causes in a year. This might be a specific charity, organisation or a business forum, but will allow you to focus proper energy on your chosen cause.

You want to ensure that your company's CSR policy is recognised and is seen to be effective. This also does not necessarily mean parting with cash (although most causes appreciate this). Other value you can consider providing may be time, resources, or even old equipment such as computers and monitors (probably written down in your accounts over time).

It is refreshing to be asked for a resource other than cash. It shows empathy for the donor and intelligence from the recipient in saying: *These are our real needs, can you help?*

> *Doing nothing for others is the undoing of ourselves.*
> — Horace Mann

The Gift of time

Many worthwhile organisations in your community only want the gift of time. I have always argued that money can be recovered; time cannot, so spend this most valuable commodity with great care.

The time they need from you may be in the form of business advice or mentoring, help with projects, or someone to serve on their Board as a Trustee. This is fulfilling work and well worth the trouble.

I have found that much of the help needed comes naturally to a business leader, and can mean tasks you normally undertake every day as a matter of routine can be repeated for a charitable cause.

Applying this to a charity, as an example (because they are a business as well), is not usually breaking new ground and can be easier and more rewarding than you might suppose.

Morale building

Other business organisations have added value by introducing a team-building day at their chosen charity to complete a task, such as a building redecoration, garden make-over or a fund-raising event. This could create a great opportunity to gain value for your team's morale, whilst also giving something back to your community.

Positive outcomes

I have no doubt that you will not be clambering to the door to give away all your hard earned gains, merrily waving your company cheque book in your hand. Next time you speak to your accountant, see what can prudently be given away and what can (if appropriate) be offset against Corporation Tax. This may have the benefit to your business of giving more for less. As we know, this can't be a bad business strategy.

Initially, I did not think that the title of this chapter, *Wonky wheel*, was a very positive headline. However, the ideas that follow are positive and I hope offer some business inspiration to ensure that no wheels fall off the machine you continue, correctly, to strive to develop.

There are many ideas that could be implemented and you should consider making a few notes for your own situation on the next pages.

Your Business Planning

🕐 Are you a business *hunter* or a business *farmer*?

🕐 Is this where you want to be? If not, how can you change?

🕐 Do you enjoy your team communications?

🕐 Have you asked your team if they enjoy them too?

🕐 You have built your brand. Have you protected it thoroughly?

🕐 Is it time for an additional brand/product line/service?

🕐 How do you control production peaks and troughs to get the best from both yourself and the team? New projects could help.

🕐 Have you looked at your work environment (from entrance to desk/production floor) recently? Could it be improved in a cost-effective way? Have you cleaned your company signs?

🕐 Do you have a CSR policy? If not, should you now have one? If you do, when did you last review it?

🕐 Is your work/life balance where you want it to be? If not, what needs to change?

Chapter Five: Small may be beautiful

Small is beautiful, this can be especially true in business. It is also usually dynamic, vibrant, flexible . . . and vulnerable. Any SME director will recognise all these traits and will also know that the 'buck' stops with him or her. Margins may be tight and no one really cares if the boss does not get paid this month . . . other than the boss, of course.

The reality is that if all the participants of the company buy in to the overall objectives of your agreed business goals, then their enjoyment in taking part is likely to increase along with your profit. We all like to achieve goals, both personally and as a team.

Communicating those goals, especially in an SME environment, is vital to ensure that everyone knows what needs to be done, what hurdles they are likely to encounter and who else is involved in the process of your plans delivery. This is why you are now a manager of people, as well as manager of your business.

Team communication

I have to admit that verbal communications of our plans and growth aspirations with the team were never my strongest point as a manager. I am still not great at this, being more naturally inclined towards a more authoritarian approach.

However, I have learned that taking time to discuss plans and ask for views and opinions on the positives and negatives of an objective or improvement change can be very rewarding.

I recently asked each team member the following question in our regular team meeting about our company: *'If you could change one thing, what would it be?'*

The answers were revealing and compelling. Most points could be changed within a week, surprisingly cheaply. More importantly, each one mattered a lot to the person who offered it.

The team wanted:
- Colour printing of our client newsletters, rather than the 'letter type' we had always used.
- The font on our website changing to a 'cleaner' text.
- New toilet seats and better quality towels in the washrooms. (A new member of staff's fresh pair of eyes sees things nobody else does. This exercise gave our staff confidence to give their opinion and resulted in a general freshening-up of the premises.)
- Better brands of coffee and biscuits for clients.
- Flat-screen TV on the wall in the office. (This idea was rejected by other team members as likely to be a distraction.)

As you can see, these suggestions were not taxing and even seemed obvious when we thought about them. It was evident that these issues mattered to the individual putting the point forward and that he or she cared about them.

It probably also mattered to our patrons who would be using these facilities. Each point was an easy win, which could be implemented quickly, offering low cost change that would improve our workplace environment, client proposition and service offering.

Team game

As we have developed our business and circumstances have changed, we have seen changes in personnel. Starting from a team of two and then growing the team numbers has been an interesting and sometimes frustrating task. In the end, though, it has been worth it.

Growing the team to give yourself more time to drive the business forward, especially during the positive economic change curve, is vital. Delegating work provides you with thinking time, to evaluate the needs of the business and the way it can move forward.

Where you are the driving force in the business, it is likely that most of the business thinking will fall to you. You have to think around issues and opportunities, even diversifications, and, more importantly, be able to convey this development information to the right people to get the action required in the way you expect.

An unconfirmed saying attributed to Thomas Edison suggests that:
Five per cent of people think. Ten per cent think they think; and the other eighty-five per cent would rather die than think.

Thinking is the hardest work there is, which is probably the reason so few engage in it.
— Henry Ford

It is easy to get bogged down in the basic chores of a business, without allowing any real time to plan your day, the week, the quarter and for the long-term future. As I have suggested, you really only have a further twelve months before growth will take hold. Make sure you move positive business solutions forward using this time wisely.

Incentives

Giving team members the respect and space to allow them to flourish is important to ensure that you, as the business owner, get the vital commitment, feedback and information you need to drive the business.

Business is usually, and correctly, an interactive team situation. You need to share your vision to ensure that each team member understands the extent of their role and the reasons why their task needs to be achieved, in the priority required in the time set. They may require incentivising. Well, if an incentive gets the target hit, this is just an additional acquisition cost and possibly a price worth paying. Just make sure the target set is worth more than the incentive paid.

Team support

First impressions count, be under no illusions otherwise. You will always represent *yourself* first and *then* the company you own. From your high quality business card, to your website address, to your attire, they all communicate your values.

Your customer-facing team also represents your company. They may be expected to dress in a particular way, such as smart business attire. For non-client facing staff, this may be less a requirement and more of an expectation.

Allowing this latter group some non-financial benefits strengthens rapport and commitment. In our business, we have started a process of allowing team members the opportunity to dress casually on the occasional Friday. Also the gift of time seems to have a greater value to many people than extra salary (although I am sure they would prefer both).

Frederick Herzberg was a psychologist who theorised that job satisfaction and job dissatisfaction act independently of each other. His catchily-named 'motivation-hygiene theory' and 'dual-factor theory' studied 'hygiene factors' such as status, job security, salary, fringe benefits and work conditions.

Among other things, he noted that salary and income is *not a motivator*. Allowing our staff an hour off on a Friday afternoon if all the day's trade is done *is* a great incentive. We make it clear that at our busy times, staying late at no cost to us would help the business and they also understand and help with this. In return, we give time to them elsewhere, where available.

Don't forget training! But for whom?

I hope you have given your team the benefit of your commercial wisdom from your prior learning before the company started. This wisdom will have been accumulated over the years to a level that gave you the confidence to go it alone, or to start your enterprise with partners.

Passing on your acumen is usually a pleasure. It allows others to develop skills and reveal talents that may be of great value to your growing business and its future strength. If you came from a large corporate environment, you may have had 'training days' crammed into your busy diary. That is certainly how I remember it and, in hindsight, I am very grateful for those opportunities.

Training can be expensive and may have to be limited in the 'incubator phase' of your new company, waiting for the maturity ahead. Now may well be the time to invest in training again.

As an overhead, training is usually one of the first to be cut when times get tough. This is likely to be a short sighted saving, especially now, when it's time to grow.

Your profession, trade or industry will continue to develop and I am sure you will have training demands from individuals looking to expand their skills repertoire to add benefit to your business. There are usually many varieties of training, and picking your options wisely can save costs, both in terms of cash and, more importantly, time spent.

With work flowing over your desk or computer screen every day, it is easy for you as the entrepreneur to lose touch with changes and innovations that could enhance your own offering. This may slow or delay development and keep you lagging behind the change curve.

Make sure that *you* take the time to take some training yourself, and to read the trade press to see what changes are being created. Both are great opportunities.

Housekeeping . . . all part of the end game

Housekeeping sounds rather mundane. It usually is. This does not detract from its necessity and importance in maintaining a healthy company as it continues its development, growth and success. It's like having your car serviced: never exciting, but it's essential to maintain your vehicle (and business) in preparation for future needs.

Every year the annual 'renewables' of insurance and regulation registration (if required) will land on your desk requiring your attention. Not all regulation is mere red tape. Some can have the benefit of protecting your profession or trade, keeping standards high and even keeping rogue traders at bay.

Take the opportunity to gain a comparison on insurance costs to make sure that this overhead remains competitive. The accompanying invoices, will not surprise you, conveniently need paying in twenty-eight days or so. You will aim to pay these as late as possible (twenty-seven days works for me!) to give the benefit of cash flow to you, rather than to the requesting recipient. You will have your own system of achieving this payment delay. I use an invoice rotation system visited once a week, which I find simple, effective, robust and time saving.

That small but vital local supplier

Assuming you are up to speed with business cash flow, you should find yourself at an advantage as you move into the future. Sadly, many of the small, but vital suppliers that you use may still be reliant on the quick settlement of any invoice they send. They do not have the financial might or sales volume of some large operations that only settle their debt accounts after ninety days or so.

Nevertheless, as a supporter of local commerce, you will want them to be around in a month's time and in a year's time to supply your business with the smaller 'keep-you-going commodities' that keep the wheels of your business turning. Paying them promptly is the lifeblood of their trade and vital to their future existence.

If you want them there in a year's time, then pay them promptly.

A reputation as a late payer will only catch you out later on, just when *you* need some local support, service and flexibility.

Holistic planning

Above all of these, you should also keep an eye on your holistic housekeeping, to keep the business in the best of health and prepared for any future outcome.

As a financial planner helping many SME and partnership owners, I could write pages at this stage about the types of protection needed and the issues that a business could face and needs to be prepared for. Rather than do this, I have suggested some headlines that are worthwhile re-visiting if you have not addressed them recently.

It would be pointless to build such a valuable asset (possibly the most valuable asset you own) as your company and not protect it. You insure your car and its contents, and they are likely to have a lower value than your established and mature business. This oversight could easily be a reflection of your hard work and success, especially when we know that positive economic change has already started.

- **Wills**

  Have you made a will? If you have assets abroad, do you have a will in that country? This is one way to confirm where your shareholding or business assets will be passed to in the event of your death. If you have co-owners or business partners, do they have valid wills and do you know who will own their share if they die?

- **Shareholder protection**

  It is possible to protect your shareholding value in the event of your death. You may already have achieved this, hopefully with some good financial planning, in the past. However, your company value is likely to have grown in its trajectory to its real future sale price. Is your current cover in line with this new value?

You should seek legal and financial advice on instituting this planning to make sure that, if needed, the transition of value works efficiently.

- **Key Person protection**

  You are a *Key Person*. We know this. What of your other key personnel, the people that keep your show on the road, and without whom the machine you have created would slow to a halt? Identify them and consider insuring their positions.

- **Illness protection**

  Your role is stressful. It has its benefits, sure, but not without corresponding business pressures. If you, or senior colleagues, were unable to work due to ill health, the burden of their salary or income may still need to be paid and this could easily be a strain on your company's cash flow. You may need to pay their salary, whilst also paying someone to stand in for them. If the health situation is serious, this may continue for many months. Not the best cash-flow position, I am sure you would agree. Suitable protection can usually be sourced to help if this were to occur.

Do not forget that medical insurance can also be established to offer provision in the event of medical care being required. At the same time, you may want to think about having a medical check-up once a year. A lot is being asked of you day-to-day, and to be blunt, no one wants you dying at your desk. That would be sad and pointless, but this situation is not unheard of. Do not let it happen to you. Your car has to have an MOT every year, why wouldn't you?

- **Diversification of savings**
  Many people suggest that their home or their business (or both) are their retirement funds. In your business, you are likely to have a few business lines or income sources to feed the company and give diversification of remuneration, profit and sustainability.

This means that you are not reliant on one source for success, if this source suffers a downturn (or even worse, stops). This diversification allows your business to be protected from potential calamity. Effectively, you would normally aim to put more than one 'horse' in your production race.

The same principle should be applied to your future retirement income. If you get it right, the sale of your business will provide you with enough funding to see you into your twilight. Any additional savings, such as pension schemes or personal savings, could be a bonus that can be used however you see fit. If it goes wrong, these additional savings may buy you time to correct any downturn in company progress or profits, or cushion the fall if the company fails.

Many business owners planning to retire at the end of the first decade of the twenty-first century will attest to this situation and the need to keep going for another five to ten years to ride out the recession we have just endured.

The notes above are not an exhaustive housekeeping list. There are many other issues to consider each year. These notes should give an indication of what you, as the company's leader, may want to revisit when moving into your next phase of business growth.

As a minimum, with the housekeeping in order, this should provide greater confidence in pushing your business further and faster.

Please note that no financial or legal advice is provided in the text of this book. Seek advice from a regulated professional for your own individual circumstances.

Freedom to find time . . . get an apprentice

I would recommend to any business owner or manager that they buy themselves and their company more time by hiring an apprentice or two.

Hiring an apprentice (or having a full apprenticeship programme) has many virtues and gives our younger people the opportunity to experience the work environment and hopefully thrive under its influence.

We started an apprentice programme just over a year ago with our local college. Our new joiner, Jack, studying an NVQ Business Administration course, has brought much energy to the team and he has relished the opportunity to get involved in the basic administration tasks required in our office, every day.

I have found that this has given the team more time to take control of other tasks, which were sometimes being rushed to meet deadlines. This in turn has taken more work away from my own desk, freeing up valuable time for creative thinking and planning. Frankly, this should be what I should be doing — and among other things, it has given me the time to think about the content of this book.

An apprentice is a cost-effective solution to freeing up time and one I would recommend. Jack has now moved on to our permanent staff and we are looking to replicate the process.

There are some who suggest that this is a way of conscripting low cost labour; I think not. Both Jack and I would agree that this is not true, at least in our experience.

I did not go to university when most people did at the age of eighteen, and only really discovered academia in my late twenties. I too started as an apprentice and just the experience of being in a work environment, allowing the business world and its systems to wash over me, was beneficial.

My personal learning curve was massive and was achieved in the mid-1980s, interestingly just as the country was coming out of recession. I think at the time the UK did not know it was coming out of a recession; only the late '80s revealing the ugly side of excess later on, which most seemed to enjoy. This '80s history records show that an economic 'cold' (and a mild one at that) was at the time only around three years away — although most people you could ask have forgotten this shallow recession, its long-term effects being generally neutral.

Youthful energy

Think about this apprentice opportunity and the energy that young people can bring to your organisation's future. Of course, they will take some time to settle in and will require suitable training. However, they are keen to get on, just like you are and were. You can mould them to meet your business needs.

These people are your company's future and all businesses need them to achieve true growth potential.

> *Youth is the trustee of prosperity.*
> — Benjamin Disraeli

Your Business Planning

⏱ Assuming you have been cautious in recruiting so far, is it now time to expand to meet market demands? How will you do this?

⏱ Would introducing an apprentice programme add value? What work could they take from you to give you more time?

⏱ What training strategy do you have in place? When was this last updated?

⏱ Do you feature in this training programme yourself?

⊘ When did you last review the corporate structure of your company and its protection needs?

⊘ Are you assured that you have protected the legal ownership of your business rights?

⊘ Would it be worthwhile having your business valued now? This could allow you to monitor value progress in the future.

Chapter Six: Never re-brand . . . oops!

I noted in my first book that re-branding, in my 'learned' opinion at the time, was not a great idea if it was not needed.

It is with some irony that following this, we unwittingly and unwillingly undertook a trade mark dispute to protect our brand; following the successful conclusion of this matter, a re-brand followed within just twenty-four months of laying down my pen from my first *Churchouse Chronicles*.

Life, and especially business life, is full of testing challenges and new experiences, and this proved to be one of them.

I had believed at the outset of my new company that having my family name anointed across the door lintel would bring the personal touch that everyone would trust and buy. This is true and it did work well — but in itself creates another problem later in the life cycle of the company.

> *Your brand is what people say about you when you're not in the room.*
> — Jeff Bezos, founder of Amazon

All businesses have a life cycle. Where is your company in its own 'life cycle' at the moment? When you come to sell your business, what is a new owner buying: you, or the business, or both?

So, what happened to us?

Fax for you, sir!

In securing our original trade mark, I had not remembered that we had signed up for an automated fax service from the Intellectual Property Office (IPO) to notify us of when an application was received applying to use a similar name in our 'class', which in our case is *UK retail financial services*.

I am sure we will have paid extra for this service, and it proved to be well worth the expense. The fax in our office chirped into life and there, emblazoned on the newly produced pages before me, was a trademark application very similar to our name, in the same class, by a large financial institution.

Thanks to my colleagues' hard work on the internet, the full terms of the reason for the application were downloaded and interrogated. This included the document and agreement with which the firm in question would register the trade mark.

Looking back, I remember us thinking we could not believe our 'luck'. How wrong we were, although the final results were worth the effort and time we invested. I am pleased this episode was concluded.

After the subsequent terms were negotiated, we successfully planned and executed a name change and re-brand. I think I was more concerned about the agreed re-brand and name change than my clients were. Communication was the key in ensuring a smooth transition from old name to new.

> *Life isn't about finding yourself. Life is about creating yourself.*
> — George Bernard Shaw

Building on the strength of our brand

My view and strategy is that in the longer term, by changing the company's name, we have maintained the strength and integrity of the old brand that we have already grown.

This involved keeping the logo similar in shape, style and colour to the old logo. However, we took the opportunity to add a more modern twist to the presentation and delivery. Both graphics and the general dynamism of our business have improved significantly over the last decade and this has proved to be a great way to reflect these changes in an upgrade and modernisation of the brand image.

As a mind-set change and an emotional 'distancing' from the company I still admire, the re-brand has been a great success. I now feel that I can sell *the business* in the distant future, rather than *the business and its owner*, namely me. You still love your business and want to stay with it, but there is now a remoteness that will never be recovered. It almost feels like an unfaithful partner you have forgiven.

At the time of writing this text, some eighteen months after the name change and new-brand alignment, the net effect has been an uplift in business. My fear was that clients would desert our organisation because my eponymous name had been removed from the door.

In fact, the removal of my name just turned out to be the end of an ego trip. No one seemed overly concerned, as long as consistent service could be maintained and renewed.

This process also allowed us to look at our overall marketing model and its delivery, to see if these needed to be updated at the same time. You will see from the notes below that there was much change to achieve.

Cleansing process

When you start a new business, you naturally endeavour to ensure that everything is in order before you throw your doors open to the buying public. This approach is only correct if you have profitability in mind. Each aspect of the delivery of your product or service represents you and the value you proffer. You should want your clients and customers to buy into your perception of the feel, quality and delivery of your unique product or service. You want that delivery to be special and personal, so much so, that those who enjoy your offering will return time and time again, telling their own contacts and connections about you along the way. Recommendations are powerful business generators.

> *Your Premium brand had better be delivering something special, or it's not going to get the business.*
> — Warren Buffett

Never underestimate the power of the word-of-mouth. I always maintain that getting the first sale from a new client is the hardest; subsequent sales are a re-affirmation of the first experience, making it easier for them to choose to buy from you again. This has the advantage of lower marketing cost per sale and usually a higher spend level.

Always remember that good news travels fast, but bad news (say, about poor service or a disappointing product) travels supersonic!

Feel your product

This raises the question: *When did you last re-assess the delivery and feel of your product?* This might be appropriate now because the market has moved on or because, after a few years trading, your proposition could have become stale.

In running a UK retail financial services advice business, a great deal of paperwork and marketing literature is produced to meet regulatory requirements and to give clients confidence in what we can do for them, both now and into the future.

For the re-brand, all our stationery had to be reprinted with the new name and logos. This was not a bad thing, because it gave me the opportunity to revisit the promotional text, which had last been proof-read some three years earlier. It is amazing how time moves on; I cringed reading parts of the 'old' marketing text, for both its delivery style and its messages. Following a full scale rewrite, fresh documents were produced to reflect our new improved and more mature proposition.

This had further consequences: we replaced and improved our signage and also looked at the office décor, website and even the machines we used, each being upgraded where required.

I was horrified when the old fax machine broke down and a staff member said it needed to be replaced. Engrossed in the pages of a document I was writing, I muttered that, *'it's only six months old'* and that *'it should still be under warranty'*. The prompt riposte was: *'The warranty ran out in 2005'*, a sign that the last seven or so years really had flown by quickly. It was clear that some attention to detail on the infrastructure of the office might be in order.

The overdue upgrade of most things in the office was refreshing, not only for me, but also the others in the office. History shows that change can have many benefits, as we have seen in Chapter Four (*Elton Mayo*).

> *Without deviation from the norm, progress is not possible.*
> — Frank Zappa

Data security and upgrades

Protecting intellectual property usually involves upgrading the security of your computer and internet facilities. Like the fax machine mentioned earlier, computer equipment and the operating systems each device uses, rapidly becomes dated, even obsolete. I think we have been through three different operating systems since we started the company; each change takes production time and management to acclimatise to.

These changes do, however, bring their benefits. First of all, they provide the platform to upgrade hardware and software to ensure that the protection of our corporate and client data improves. This is vital because as we all know, the various new types of 'phishing and hacking' have also developed, as many large multinational computer-based producers have seen to their cost in recent times.

It is also a chance to review hardware providers and the way systems are acquired — comparing purchase versus the option of leasing — to ensure that value and accounting efficiencies are maintained.

'Culling' clients

Naturally, I mean this from a business profitability point of view, rather than literally. It is something that does not come naturally to an acquisitive business getter, but it is absolutely necessary to maintain margins. Your aim at the outset of your business is to create a loyal customer/client base that will use you again and again into the future. As you mature, you may then segment this customer or client base to maintain and enhance profit. (I will say more about the segmentation process later in this chapter.)

Large retailers are keen on target marketing using technology, such as loyalty cards. This concept can be expensive to apply and even unaffordable to smaller SMEs. Additional applied thinking and manual monitoring may be a more realistic alternative to achieve effective and profitable segmentation. You could also consider using the latest data mining services/ techniques (a fascinating subject in its own right), in this case for target marketing, to improve corporate messaging and results.

Initially, it was not a profit motive that made our business look at client segmentation; it was increased regulation and this cost that focused our minds. Ultimately, these do lead to a profit perspective.

Regulation and red tape are the bane of many mature economies, especially in the developed western hemisphere. Irrespective of the industry you are in, health and safety, banking regulation, tax rules and alike will slow down you and your business, as you spend time ticking boxes to keep someone you will never meet in a job.

In the modern 'digital by default' world that now envelops us all, we usually submit these forms online. This then generates an invoice that includes no explanation as to why the amount has gone up by more than inflation with no visible benefit to the business. The cost of your or your staff's time in complying with this regulation has to be borne by the company and factored into the price point offered to enquirers and existing clients.

As a business, a significant regulation change forced us to review our business model and the services we provided. The 'red tape' applied by our regulator was significant, correctly raising the professional 'bar' in almost all directions.

Although this seemed unhelpful in many ways, it did make us drill down into our client offering and review the real unit cost to the business of providing each of our services. I recently heard this referred to as a *deep dive*, going to the very bottom of the sales and cost process and evaluating the effect on profitability as you ascend to completion of the transaction. It was a revealing exercise, which demonstrated minimum cost delivery and also highlighted the accumulated and increasing overheads that now had to be factored in.

Minimum pricing policy

Overnight we introduced and promoted a minimum starting cost to purchase our services. Any request made to offer service below this agreed remuneration level (which increases by five per cent per annum from there onwards for protection against inflation) would be declined.

This has had various effects. The number of new enquiries went down, saving us time by not talking to prospects who would not place true value on our proposition and business acumen. It also meant that any enquirers to whom we did speak were aware of our costs and fees and were usually happy with the transparency of these, even before they arrived at our premises for the first meeting.

We started attracting a different calibre of enquirer. They had usually accumulated more wealth because of their attitude to life and work, and this increased the value of the business we transacted.

The fact that such people already value our service before they arrive makes the sales and delivery process more relaxed and professional. The more relaxed both parties are, the more business they usually undertake.

Now that you have been running your business for a while and it is out of its infancy, and you have accumulated the necessary data of what a good, bad and indifferent customer or client looks like, have you recalculated the minimum spend that each client needs to achieve to make the business your transact profitable?

I have to admit that I had never undertaken a calculated review before in my company. It is easy to see now that I was clearly undercharging in certain situations, hence the necessity for a new minimum starting price.

This might just be a simple way of applying the 80:20 rule: that twenty per cent of your clients give you 80 per cent of the profit. It does take a disciplined approach. You may lose less profitable customers on the way — although you can always make exceptions if they are important to you.

In my experience, it does move you up the income scale and personally gives greater satisfaction, knowing that you are being rewarded appropriately for the work that you and your colleagues secure and that your clients value.

Business segmentation

We also looked at our existing customer base. In the early years, we took on any type of business to get the income rolling. We started in early October with the first income making it to our bank account in November. We joked that, *'there would be butter on our parsnips'* that Christmas. With most of our capital deployed in our new business, that's pretty much all we got.

In reviewing the client data at business maturity, we found that around thirty per cent of our client base offered very low levels of income, with the majority of the business income coming from the top thirty per cent.

Interestingly close to the archetypal 80:20 business profit rule noted above.

We then undertook a process of engaging with the thirty per cent of clients who were in the 'Low-Profit' catergory, offering them three levels of service at three fixed cost points or the option to pay nothing and for us to disengage. The offer to return to us at some future time was left open.

The results of the process are noted on Page 101, *Politely disengage*.

Politely disengage

All of the clients identified in the low profit/no profit segment took the opportunity to disengage, because they did not want to pay for our services. Is this because they did not value our service? Possibly! We are not running a business as a charity (even though charitable organisations are correctly becoming more business savvy) and if we are going to grow profitability, we have to concentrate on those clients that can and are happy to value the services we offer.

The segmentation process reduced costs and time spent on contacting unprofitable clients, freeing time and thinking space to concentrate on enhancing our service to the identified profitable clients.

As the business owner or director, it is your role to influence the business. When, like me, you hit a production ceiling, it is time to put on your thinking cap and identify the way that this imaginary production ceiling can be shattered. Client segmentation and differentiation is one effective solution, as long as it is handled with care and consideration.

Your Business Planning

🕐 What does your brand say about you and your enterprise?

_____

_____

_____

_____

🕐 Is your brand still as dynamic as the company it represents?

_____

_____

_____

_____

🕐 Have you segmented your client or customer base to see how you achieve sales, profit and income?

_____

_____

_____

_____

🕐 When did you last dissect the costs of completing a sale or deal?

_____

_____

_____

_____

🕐 As a percentage, what was the margin of profit? What was your target margin?

_____

_____

_____

_____

🕐 Could this margin be increased by reducing costs or increasing prices/number of units/additional sales per consumer?

_____

_____

_____

_____

🕐 When did you last look at your marketing literature and update it? Does it reflect your vision now?

_____

_____

_____

_____

🕐 What is your marketing plan for the next five years? Why?

_____

_____

_____

_____

⏲ What is your PR plan for the next five years? What made you agree this plan?

_____

_____

_____

_____

⏲ Why do you believe each plan will work in a growth economy?

_____

_____

_____

_____

Chapter Seven: Accounting, money and cash flow

I am a Chartered Financial Planner by profession. This may not have been the most dynamic of professions in the past, but it is now improving enormously, delivering worthwhile and satisfying financial plans to individuals, directors and SMEs.

Under my belt are some twenty-eight years of service in UK financial services, eight of them in my own SME. I am not an accountant, but we both deal with money and figures. As a business owner, I am acutely aware of cash flow.

I did study Accounts at our local college for a very short period, and as you can guess by the duration of my study, I was not strong at this subject at the time. Clearly, my interest lay elsewhere. Of course, I could find my way round a set of company or personal accounts — only just — but at the time any form of detailed scrutiny was way beyond me.

This does not mean that I have somehow morphed into an expert since then. However, it is remarkable how much more interesting company accounts can be when it's your own money! Over the years, my understanding has grown and the biggest lesson is still that of *cash flow*.

Cash flow

No business, country or economy can function without cash flow. You should already know this from balancing your home budget to your commercial budget. When there is no cash, you are not going very far.

We have seen US politicians fighting over what to do about their *Fiscal Cliff*. Very simply put, this is an argument about whether the country can and should extend their borrowing limit by a few more trillion dollars to pay for their current deficit, infrastructure repairs and future lifestyles. I am not sure that they have many options, but reduction in spending is one of them. The outcome is likely to be a mixture of the two solutions — borrowing to invest, and cutting spending.

Some commentators refer to any resolution that includes raising the borrowing limits as 'kicking the can down the road' (putting the problem forward for a few years so that it does not have to be addressed today).   A very apt term for this position. Do not let your company get into the same situation.

Margins

Many economic principles apply equally to businesses, SMEs or larger national and global organisations. In principle, and in my opinion, there are only two basic things that a business owner can do to improve profit and cash flow. This is either to increase sales or reduce costs. Both would be preferable.

The gap created by these parameters, increased sales versus reduced costs, should eventually lead to profit. However, you need *cash* in the meantime to do this. There is usually an acquisition cost involved in sales. If you cannot afford the acquisition cost, you probably cannot increase sales. You have to buy or create goods and services to be able to sell them on at a profit.

When you started the business, I am sure you prepared a business plan, which looked at these very points. When is the last time you revisited them? Or looked at your business plan, assuming you have one?

Sales and cost reduction targets

You annually set yourself a sales/income or production target. This is only natural and good business practice. Addressing this can provide both you and your staff with a focus. There should never be a problem in sharing with the team what you want to get done, how they can help, and when it needs to be done by.

Do you want to be the *best* company or the *most profitable* company? The two do not necessarily match up, although offering a good quality product may more easily lead to regular and sustainable profitability than a low quality or low price approach.

Each approach is likely to attract different classes of end consumer and different cost and profit outcomes. I am sure you need little guidance on setting an achievable production target for the year and to calculate the potential profit you will strive for.

Cost reduction targets

Likewise, have you ever set yourself a *cost reduction* target alongside your business production target?

Take a step back from your business and look at your natural business expenditure. You may well find that some cost 'excess' has been accumulated. You might want to see it as a middle age 'spare tyre' of cost that, with a bit of exercise, could be removed. Try it!

Well managed businesses of all sorts do this. Whether they refer to it as a *comprehensive spending review* (yet another CSR acronym), or just a *budget review meeting*, the principles are the same.

I feel that if I can sell £10,000 of services in a week, that's great. This might be high or low compared to your own business model, so please translate this amount to your own circumstances. If I can save £10,000 of costs in another week, this will have the same effect of increasing our profit margin. Both will increase your ability to move forward and both are well worth achieving.

To gear or not to gear, that is the question

New projects, new product lines and innovations use up development cash and, on starting a new initiative, your business can find a lot of your hard earned money flowing out of the door with nominal initial return. Your business plans should reflect this.

This business investment is usually arranged with the plan that the cost-versus-benefit will be worthwhile, over time. It's just a question of how long and to what extent this project provides returns. The equation could read: Cost/Time over Return.

You could use your own accumulated cash, or borrow for the project, or part-and-part to deliver the required outcome. The main issue with this notion is that many of the usual lenders that businesses have relied on in the past, mainly the banks, have been slow in offering finance at the right time.

Borrowing to develop is worthwhile considering, although the additional borrowing cost should be offset against the potential profit to ensure your planning remains viable.

Opportunity cost

My personal view, and this is *not* advice, is that a business should carry some borrowing, or *gearing,* as it is sometimes known.

If this capital is not immediately deployed, it can be held in an interest-bearing account, offsetting the borrowing cost. It does not take a genius to work out that the differential between the two is a cost to the business. This is sometimes referred to as an *opportunity cost*.

Many banks and deposit takers can offer businesses various savings options, such as money markets accounts, but they are not that proactive in doing so.

If you have secured the finance whilst it is available, you may then plan to hold it to use when you are ready. Yes, you are paying interest in the meantime, however, you will not have to approach the lender when the project demands it — the money will be ready and waiting.

Bearing in mind that many recent bank lending policies extend all the way from, *No! What was the question again?* to *We will lend you a little bit, but only when it suits us,* taking finance when it's available can have benefits, admittedly at a cost to your immediate profits. You will need to take individual advice on your own circumstances before borrowing.

New lenders have come to the fore in recent years. These include Venture Capitalists and, to a lesser extent, Business Angels. Each has its place in the market; however, they are not charities and are in this for profit. There is nothing wrong with that, as long as you pay special attention to the terms of the deal that is being proffered. If it looks too good to be true . . . it usually is.

This text is not a case of 'bank bashing', that popular pastime of recent years. It just faces the reality that many banks are struggling with their own cash flow and regulatory capital adequacy issues. This can mean that an SME director like you or me cannot access the capital he or she needs to get a project off the ground, irrespective of how good the proposition is.

This does not help business managers in planning productivity into the future. Innovative projects for many businesses have been put on hold merely in order to control costs, sadly negating demand for employment, growth and profits.

Project timing

When you make a change to your business model, such as expansion or a change in sales focus, make sure that you have sufficient cash flow to support the change.

As a business experience, our company moved from a *commission* model to a *fee based* model in 2007. I still struggle to remember how this decision came about; however, it has proved to be both fortuitous and profitable in the long run for a number of reasons.

For our business, there was an income lag over the first six month period, where cash flow fell, but work in progress increased during that time. The net effect was a pregnant business pipeline and a slow cash intake. As a business owner, you may know how painful this can be but this is exactly the point, be ready for this.

My message is simple: you know when the peak performance months are in your business year and you know when the company bank accounts are at their fittest. If you are going to make positive change to enhance performance and innovation (at the possible cost of cash flow in the short term), then start the project at the time when you have the most cash to see you through to the reward phase. Revisit old years' production charts to get your timing right.

Coming of age

You may experience a situation where your company becomes more successful because times change and the market for your goods or services simply moves towards you. Enjoy this if and when it happens.

We have certainly experienced this with our own online-based product offering which, until a recent legislation change, had seen little activity, with only continuing cost rather than profit. We reviewed the offering regularly to ascertain if the product might be misplaced, was never really going to work or, more positively, could be a situation that it would have its day, eventually! I am pleased to note that our internet based product line employed an '*Economy of Scope*' principal, as noted in the book.

It is important to be both realistic, and to some extent ruthless, if the need to cut your losses and jettison a project or product is the only honest outcome. An alternative to this is to 'park' a project, stopping any further development or management time at one point and seeing whether external changes make it worth reintroducing the product or service later.

In scrutinising the viability and profitability of the product in question, do you need to do this *now*? Or would the energy that will need to be focused to succeed be better channelled elsewhere, for the time being at least?

Never be concerned about taking either action if the time is simply wrong. Where a project or innovation is fundamentally good, it will come of age and will have its profit point. Timing, sometimes, can be everything.

Sweating assets

I had not heard of the term *sweating assets* until around a year ago — probably because I had not needed this strategy before. Many corporates are undertaking this planning successfully to reduce costs. We have already seen the value in it.

As our business has matured, the usage of our business assets, from office space to team members, has increased as the flow of commerce has increased. Sometimes, the need to expand is there, but the will to increase expenditure has been limited because of the volatility in business conditions and the availability of cash flow and finance (as we noted earlier).

You may not want to commit to increased office space, even on a short term lease, on the back of the potential upturn, in case this turns out to be an unexpected blip.

Looking at and re-deploying assets to meet demand has worked well for many in recent times to achieve profitable outcomes. Working assets harder or smarter without increasing costs can be highly valuable. There is a limit to the number of times you can do this before the asset itself fails.

Squeeze tight

This *sweating* of assets has developed a long way in some businesses, where existing companies have previously enjoyed spacious office accommodation. They have then moved into smaller areas within their existing facilities to sub-let floor space to other companies to reduce fixed costs, such as rent and business rates. In successful instances, this has allowed other costs, such as administration, catering and energy costs, to be shared, increasing profits for both organisations.

These are only examples. Many parts of a business, from marketing to stationery, can be 'sweated' if you look at them carefully.

We have also seen larger companies and businesses *merging* with smaller companies to share costs, client bases and professional indemnity costs. Again, profitable . . . as long as it works.

As you can guess, extracting yourself from such a *merger* can be costly if it goes wrong.

This raises the question as to what a *merger* really is?

There's no such thing as a merger

A financial agreement between two parties to join each other can be dressed up with any name you want: merger, sale or takeover. That is what the public relations and marketing people are there for. They will give any change a positive spin — and the world would not spin without a bit of . . . well . . . *spin*.

There are many examples of national brands that *merge* with others, forming a double-barrelled business name only for the lesser party name to be dropped after a couple of years. Was this a merger after all? You decide.

The reality is that there is usually one party that gains and one party that concedes. This should not be a problem, as long as it is carefully managed and egos do not run away with any of the parties involved.

It is prudent to be mindful of this position in any earn-out situation, where you move from decision-maker to decision-taker in quick succession. This change may work for you financially, but from a day-to-day work environment process, it may not be so favourable.

In some cases, the sale price agreed depends on future profitability. Be prepared to see this change through to make the outcome as profitable and positive as possible. This outcome may be subject to your client's reaction and interaction with your enterprise.

You have a choice . . . and so does everyone else

When was the last time you changed a business contract provider, big or small?

This change would have been for two reasons. The main reason would be to improve things such as costs, quality, style, content, speed of delivery, contact or professionalism. Something would have tipped you over the edge to say: '*This point has got to change*'. This may have taken you out of your comfort zone in disappointing an existing provider, but once the final straw has been laid upon you, there are few things that can stop you from changing.

The second reason is because you have choice as to where you place your business contracts. It is up to you to exercise that choice.

Think about this a stage further. The buyers of your services can do the same. Competitors are likely to want to entice these 'profit centres' away from you with special offers and promises of enhanced service. Ideas, such as a regular company newsletter as an example, may stop the potential for this interference by providing reminders of the good things you do. You will not find it hard to write a page on your business, which should be after all, your passion.

If an individual or company has moved away from your service or product, and you had the opportunity, did you ask why? What tipped them over the edge to look elsewhere and move away?

It is not the employer who pays the wages.
Employers only handle the money. It is the customer who pays the wages.
— Henry Ford

Unsatisfactory outcome

Take a moment to think about the last company you dealt with in your business that disappointed you. You will know why, at the end of your interaction, you felt the way you did. Have you applied this thinking to your *own* business and its product or service? Would you walk away satisfied with the outcome of your own companies interactions?

I am not suggesting you conduct a 'mystery shop', although many business owners and larger companies do. However, it is better for you to find the flaws in your offer . . . before the end user does.

Survey?

When was the last time you surveyed your clients or offered them a facility to give feedback on your business offering? This, of course, may introduce some risk (especially if you are a heavily regulated business) but will have the benefit of telling you a few home truths that you may not want to hear. Yes, I have used the word 'benefit' here correctly.

If you have habitually sold a tangible product, designed to suit an identified client need, be mindful that the end consumers' needs do evolve and change. Forget this fact and they will go elsewhere to meet those changing needs.

If the feedback hurts and is uncomfortable, it is probably a good thing and a real opportunity to improve your delivery. The process may increase short term costs, but the profit gain in working with your end users and demonstrating that you value their opinion is likely to be worthwhile.

Asking for opinion always leaves you open to criticism and you need to be prepared for this. After all, you are in a way asking your end user to detail your shortcomings. *Doing something that scares you every day* may well place you outside your comfort zone — and this is a good thing. When you step outside this zone regularly enough, two things are likely to happen: you will learn from the honest feedback and you will extend the scope of your comfort zone. Both are positive outcomes.

> *Your most unhappy customers are your greatest*
> *source of learning.*
> — Bill Gates

Your Business Planning

🕐 Do you speak to your professional advisers regularly to ensure you are getting best value from them and your business assets?

🕐 When was the last time you did this? What did you agree?

🕐 Do you scrutinise your cash flow to note income peaks and pinch points? How do you record these?

🕐 Could the physical business assets you maintain be worked harder or differently to increase revenue and profit? Would changes reduce costs?

⊘ When are you planning your next project start? Does this correlate with your peak cash in-flow months?

⊘ Could your business assets be sold or changed to evolve and enhance production techniques?

⊘ If prudent and available, would corporate borrowing now be worthwhile to gear production sales for your future targets?

⊘ Could any non-core cash accumulated in the business work harder for you whilst you decide what you are going to do with it?

🕐 Could any of your business assets be 'sweated' harder or differently to create more profit?

_____

_____

_____

_____

🕐 Do you survey your clients/customers? How, and is this the most effective way of getting the real feedback you need to improve and develop?

_____

_____

_____

🕐 Is now a time to do this? Their opinion is your profit.

_____

_____

_____

Chapter Eight: Name your price?

Imagine if, by invitation, I were to visit your business today and, after a convivial and frank discussion, offered you an acceptable price to purchase your company outright and for you to leave your desk that evening and never come back.

How much would you want? I have my imaginary cheque book ready, I have dated the cheque and I just need to know the payee and the amount. Name your price?

You are a decisive person, that is why you lead the business, and this decision should not be a problem. Should it?

Are you hesitating? If so, you need to think about the situation, because I hope your day will come. You may feel that you are not yet ready to sell off the fruits of your labour . . . yet. But when will you be ready?

Do you remember why you started your business in the first place? Was it not to build it up, gain profit and income and finally to sell it? Or was it to provide freedom to allow you to work as you want? Or was it for income? Or perhaps a mixture of them all?

I hope this aim has been achieved, but it must come to an end.

Earn out your capital

The reality of any future business sale is that a cash sum value may *not* be offered up front; there is more likely to be an *earn-out proposition* over a period of time. This might be over three years, for example, and you might want to factor this into your planned exit timing.

Bearing in mind that life is never quite so perfect that a purchaser walks in just when you want them to, it might take some time to find a suitable partner. Should this take two years, with an earn-out over three years, you are looking at a five year process. Be ready for this; your capital payments may be based on future performance and profitability, and you will need to have the energy to capitalise on the sale opportunity and proposition.

Of course, all this does not mean that you might not be one of the lucky ones who find a great buyer and a sale is completed quickly. If you are, then enjoy.

Think also about the quality of any purchaser and their proposition. You will need to be confident that they will be profitable over your earn-out period to pay you the sale capital agreed. Also, would you buy their product/service? If not, your clients may not. This may give you an uphill battle in converting clients over to the new owner. The company may have your own name above the door; as I have personally discovered, this is not always a good thing. It makes the company personal to you. This might have been a great ego trip at the outset, to see your name in lights, or in the press or even on the side of a van. Most enjoy having their ego stroked.

The reality is that this is usually not the best thing in business. It may well be a reasonable idea to get the business going — after all, people buy people, especially from SMEs and small partnerships.

However, when selling the business or professional practice in the future, what is a purchaser buying? You . . . or the business? You may feel that being wed to the business for the rest of your life has some appeal, but time and your business partners or spouse may have other ideas.

Timing is important

If you had the choice (and you usually do!) would you sell your business in a recession or at the peak of an economic cycle? With a boom economy and cash sloshing around in a buoyant market, you are more likely to get the price you want. It is like selling a convertible car: you would probably try to time this sale in the spring when the air is warming and the 'wind in your hair' experience can be enjoyed. You would not sell an open-topped car in the depth of winter, unless you were forced to.

You can plan when you sell your business, too. By returning to the boom years of the boom-bust cycle of an economy, it is likely that we will climb gradually out of recession in the next few years, start to boom and then plateau over the next five years before reaching a decline phase in the early to mid-2020s. Ten to twelve years from bust — to growth — to bust again.

You can work the rest out as to when you might want to plot your own exit process. This timing is obviously not a precise prediction, and you can freely dispute the anticipated economic progress I am suggesting. Of course there will be fiscal turbulence during this future period, but I do not think the trends will be too far away from the process and eventual outcomes as I have described them.

Hopefully, with your bank balance swollen and a successful exit negotiated and implemented, what will you do with your new found freedom?

One good way of answering this is to ask whether you have become *unemployable* during your tenure at the top. Could you return to being on the employer payroll, taking a regular salary? Even more importantly, could you go back to taking orders from others, whilst they make the business decisions that you used to make every day and possibly move you in a direction which you (and maybe your old business in an earn-out situation) may not like?

Be careful for what you wish for, because you just may get it, is a saying that springs to mind here. Even with cash in the bank, be prepared for change and its day-to-day effects.

Don't over-value your business

You have grown your business and I am sure it has proved to be a success. Long may this progress continue. Selling a business is a lot like selling a house, where *value* is just as subjective and elastic.

Many people are surprised by the amount of business capital and value they have accumulated by the time of their retirement, mainly because they have been so busy focusing on their company business that they had not seen it rise. These are the people who set out, not to make money as their priority, but to be the best at their trade or profession. A consequence of this is that these people do create significant wealth in the process.

Invariably, we all have an inflated price in mind as to what our businesses are worth. Undoubtedly you will have a unique selling point (USP) that has made the business such a success.

What is the USP for your business? Is this worth the price that you want to sell it for? Imagine you were the buyer: would *you* pay someone the asking price? If you are the originator of that business and its USP, would you pay the same price if you were not going to be there to help push the business forward?

The simple question is: *Would you pay the same amount for the business with the current owner in or out of the business?* If the answer is no, then what precisely is being sold? The inferred answer is *the owner's expertise*, which if they are retiring (or at least planning their wind-down) will only have a limited shelf life.

> *Too many people overvalue what they are not and undervalue what they are.*
> — Malcolm Forbes, Publisher

What are you going to do with all this time on your hands?

The dreaded 'R' word — retirement — may appear on the horizon at some point. It's an idea feared by many, as is the release from their beloved desk or workstation that they have hidden behind and that has protected them valiantly for years.

Freed from the battlefields of business to return home to their loved ones, is it any wonder that divorce rates in this age sector have seen the highest increase of any age group in recent years (Source: Office of National Statistics /2011).

There might also be some emotive reasons why you want to stay at your desk. You might enjoy interactions with your loyal clients with whom you have worked for years, building significant rapport that has spilt over into long-term friendships. You may not want to leave them with the potentially unknown quantity that is the new owner. I certainly have this as one of my major considerations, with some of my best clients truly relying on the service I and the company offer.

I have a client, George, who reached the 'runway' to retirement. With some three years to go until 'landing', I asked him what his plans were when he left his employer. Silence followed, then controlled sobbing for a few minutes before he composed himself and admitted that the void he anticipated could not be filled. His work had become his life, and some could argue, his life had become his work. Do not let this happen to you.

The day will come when this release is offered to you. It can be an emotional time for both you and your family, and you may want to consider a transitional period. Making sure that it is not a massive upheaval is important to ensure that you really can enjoy the fruits of your determination and hard work.

Lies, damned lies and statistics

Evan Esar's definition of statistics:
The science of producing unreliable facts from reliable figures.

Well done on starting your business all that time ago. For me, that was the biggest, and in hindsight, the most momentous hurdle I have undertaken. Do you remember closing up after the first day's trading and coming home to relate the tales of the adventure that was your first day?

My first real-life business lesson was that thinking you are good at something, starting a new business based on this assumption and then getting people to pay proper money for your product or service to make it profitable are three unique and very different achievements. Each has a separate process and needs to be accomplished successfully to proceed to the next one.

At the start of my first business in 2004, the professional consensus at the time was that you needed a business plan for three years and that on survival of the first 36 months, you would be pretty much out of the woods.

The more astute of the readers of these pages will not take long to work out the timing for our start-up. After three years, the recession, almost exactly to the day, kicked off with a vengeance. I am not sure why, I think it was misjudged naivety that made me think that after three years my business would be out of its infancy, into some level of maturity and that the trials and tribulations of getting everything up and running would abate and life would get easier. This has proved to be a misguided view.

Let us be clear: I enjoy work and always have done. Interestingly, most of the very successful people I have met enjoy work and working. They still thrive on the challenges that commerce brings and, of course, enjoy the rewards it offers. Is there a link between hard work and success? Surely not!

I remember reaching the three year trading anniversary and, in conversation with an accountant contact, being told that it was in fact the first twenty-four months that are critical. As an example of how quickly business understanding changes, the latest statistics suggest that most new businesses fail *in the first year*. I must admit to having only found this out much later.

Testing times

In my personal development, 2004 was a huge business learning curve. Planning the new structure consumed every spare moment to make sure I got it right.

To back up my business plan, I wanted to test it. I opened a bank account in preparation to trade and immediately asked the bank for an overdraft facility. I did not need one, but I wanted to see if they would lend to my new company, based on my business plan and their confidence in it. This was not a common request made of the banks at the outset of a new business (especially when you now know that most fail within the first twelve months).

The overdraft was granted and, clearly, my planning had been approved. I took some encouragement from this outcome, which gave me additional confidence that the plans and objectives really could work.

I have to add a caveat to the paragraph above in noting that this was achieved in mid-2004, long before the global banking meltdown we have seen since then. We now know that getting money out of the banks at a fair cost can prove an 'interesting' process, and I am sure they would never entertain such a frivolous application from a fresh start-up today.

Change dynamics

Business is a dynamic animal, forever changing its direction, appearance and objectives; your business should reflect and lead these changes if it wants to succeed. Hard work will see you a long way down the road to success — but with the additions of perseverance, determination and innovation, the whole journey should become smoother and quicker.

History shows, and will continue to show, that change and innovation can move rapidly. There are many examples that demonstrate this dynamism, both in product terms, types and the way they are applied by corporations.

A good example of the way a process can change completely can be found some 100 years ago. At the beginning of the 1900s, the main mode of transport was via horse power in its various forms.

There was a new 'fad' of travelling by a motor-powered vehicle, an automobile, or *car* to you and me. Just fifteen years later, cars were everywhere and horse power was consigned to history. Around sixty million cars are now made worldwide each year and their production techniques are watched, admired and copied by many non-related industries.

Just-in-time (JIT) production is one good example of development change that continues to offer producers significant unit levels, whilst keeping production and labour costs to a minimum, improving returns on investment.

A more modern change example might be the way you are reading this book. You now have the choice of a physical paperback, or the electronic e-reader version. For an amusing interlude, watch the film *Kinky Boots* by Deane & Firth (2005), based in Northampton, which demonstrates how an innovative product development changes a company and its fortunes.

In consideration of these developments, we can then also think about the ways in which each product development has been applied. Using the example at the start of this section, we can easily refer to Henry Ford and his mass production methods which proved to be such a major success, changing production thinking and the build models for cars . . . as well as most other high-production volume industries. In doing so, did he also invent consumerism? Certainly paying higher wages allowed his staff to afford to buy the very products they were making. He was not solely responsible — but he certainly enjoyed the benefits of identifying and being at the forefront of this change situation.

These changes were quick, in business terms, and revolutionary. Many now well-known names joined in at this time with varying success; others were late adopters of change and their demise invariably followed.

Likewise, fashions and trends in business, both locally and globally, change quickly. Being in touch with market developments is vital to be on or in front of the change curve. As an SME, you may not be able to influence a market with a new product innovation, such as (as an example), the production of an e-reader device. However, you could write a best-selling book to provide the content!

Intelligent application of business resources to the change process and its opportunities for your company is a sensible approach to your future prosperity.

Change still needs to happen with maturity

Having seen it through the first years and having made it to some maturity after growth, what do you want to achieve *now*? What are you going to change? Have you thought and planned the opportunities ahead?

You may still be a small and dynamic enterprise, with energy levels still high, but trading reality has now set in and day-to-day commercial decisions come easily, without rocking the brain cells too much. This has its advantages in avoiding surprises, but will you yet need to make some big directional decisions to set your future course? Have you planned these changes? Standing still is unlikely to bear dividends.

The decisions, objectives and planning you set now, and in the next twelve months, are likely to be the value you extract in the years to come.

Your Business Planning

⊙ How much would you sell your business for today?

⊙ How did you calculate this value? Why?

⊙ If you were writing the cheque yourself, would you pay someone this amount for your business/company? Why?

⊙ How do you want to structure your exit? How long will it take?

🕐 What could you change now to make the value on sale larger in the future?

🕐 What do you want to achieve once the sale is complete?

🕐 What would stop you selling your company? Why?

🕐 With the recession over and growth forecast ahead, what date in the future will your enterprise attract its maximum potential value?

🕐 How will you start the sale process?

_____

_____

_____

_____

🕐 Could a change of production/sale of your product method increase the value of the business?

_____

_____

_____

_____

Chapter Nine: If I were starting again, I would not start from here

The title of this chapter is a phrase I have often used in the last few recessionary years. It can refer to the limitations of my abilities as an SME director and also the frustration that is caused in not being further forward in the development of the organisation . . . or sometimes both! I appreciate that I am not alone in these aspirations to be further on in a company's development.

This statement also refers to the economic climate that we have all endured over the last few years, as we reach the end of recession and move into a period of sustained growth.

As a director or business owner, if you had the choice as to when to run a company, which period in the economy would you prefer: an economy in recession or in growth? With the positive outlook ahead, *now* appears to be an opportune moment. Of course, if you are running an insolvency practice, you may prefer the former economic climate.

However, the majority of directors and business owners would prefer the growth period as a backdrop to offer confidence to thrive and prosper.

We have already covered a lot of ground with many ideas, objectives and plans to consider and hopefully implement. In this penultimate chapter I will add some additional thoughts and initiatives that you may want to add on to your own planning to give you that extra *upper hand* which I aspire to achieve within my own enterprises.

Start with the end in mind

Setting out to start a small business should be exciting! As it grows, it should remain exciting. For me, finding out some eight years later that you have exactly what you set out to achieve (a small business), and then realising this is not entirely what you wanted (a medium-sized company) was frustrating. At least I hit my target. Had I known earlier what I know now, and the lessons I have noted in these pages, who knows what might have happened?

The path you set all that time ago, if run well, will lead you to where you wanted to be. Remember: *Be careful what you wish for!* Whatever you do, make sure the target you set back then is still the one you want to hit now. If not, change course now; however, plan this carefully.

If you want a medium-sized business, then set your plans accordingly at the outset and keep this plan monitored. I have said earlier that *small is beautiful*. Make sure that the 'small' you want and the 'small' you get are the same thing. You may guess that I am learning this quickly . . . now!

Communication evolution

Change, in both our personal and business lives, is happening all the time and we should embrace and lead this. Change is inevitable and will happen without us; it is just a choice as to how we engage with it.

Change is also nothing to be feared. You will know this as the leader of your enterprise. The way we engage and communicate change with other companies and individuals for commerce has also changed in recent years.

You are responsible for your business message, proposition and any changes that happen to it. I would confirm one point about this which I learned in the very first few weeks of the company: no one else is going to get your business message across as well as you and your team (unless you are paying a consultant), and real results can only be delivered by effort and energy from your own team.

Remember this lesson when you plan your communications.

> *Many a small thing has been made large by the right kind of advertising.*
> — Mark Twain

Press the flesh

It is all well and good chasing after 'New World' marketing (as I will confirm in this chapter), however, you can lose sight of the 'Old World' opportunities, which remain both valid and effective for profitable communication.

I went to an awards event in London where I was introduced to a few new people. They were polite in their introductions, not really knowing who I was. The facilitator of this introduction mentioned that I was @onlinefinancial (my Twitter name) and they beamed, having had many conversations with me consisting of fewer than 140 characters over the years. It was great to *press the flesh* and put a real face to the virtual personas that stood in the throng of the mingling crowd. It was an enjoyable, but very odd experience, almost outside the normality of the real world.

Do not let your virtual social media and marketing messages usurp the old-school approach. They should *both* work in tandem, allowing you and your team to run and attend real events as a business. You can then interact virtually with your colleagues, contacts and even your competition to generate goodwill, secure existing business and win new introductions. As I have suggested, people will always buy *people* first.

This tandem approach to real and virtual presence will take team planning and coordination to make sure that you and your team are getting the most from your applied energy.

New world marketing

How many books, blogs and 'expert' guidance can you read about navigating the universe that is *social media* and other forms of communication and networking? Each website, networking event or website and seminar has its own merits, varying in quality to your business. Some entrepreneurs swear by them . . . others swear at them!

You will have to make on-going decisions on exactly how you are involved, what time and cost you plan to deploy to each and how to manage and measure outcomes. These outcomes should be reviewed regularly to ensure that real value is being gained now, or (as part of a strategy) into the future.

My own personal experience is that each area can have greater or lesser value. There is also a very fair argument to suggest that you only get out what you put in. Standing on the side lines of social media and hoping to get referrals, orders and business is just not going to work. I would also suggest that as long as social media interaction is used sensibly and intelligently, it can be a great opportunity to raise the profile of a business, product, service or individual.

I have detailed some thoughts below for your own business communication planning and consideration.

> *Networking is an essential part of building wealth.*
> — Armstrong Williams

Networking

I remember at the start of my company going to every event and networking breakfast/lunch/drinks/dinner I could physically attend. My inexperience in gaining value from these events must have shone like a beacon. I would have foolishly gone to the opening of an envelope had I been invited. Time and my understanding of how to use these events to commercial advantage have changed.

Having declined in popularity for a while, possibly at the rise of social media, face-to-face networking seems to have become more important again to SME businesses in recent times. It is vital to have a deliberate and intelligent business marketing strategy to get the most out of the time invested by both you and your team members at these events.

When networking really started to become popular, I think many business people jumped on the bandwagon to get involved, with marginal results in many cases. This personal marketing approach then waned for a time, with some criticising the results gained. Its fortunes are now rising once more, with more emphasis on the *quality* of networking, rather than the *quantity*. This can only be a good thing and it is allowing attendees to plan what they want to gain from their attendance, who they want to meet and importantly, what they want to impart.

I have spoken to many business leaders who have said that they get more business by giving away information. You have to be ready to do business and to share ideas, innovations and plans (within reason) freely. This information can create opportunities to work together with others, to create successful affiliations and to increase business flow.

Do not get a reputation as a freeloader who is chiefly there for the free sandwiches. You will not win contacts and influence people that way. Do not sit with your colleagues; spread yourselves out. Do not chat to old friends and acquaintances when there are new faces to explore and greet. Volunteer to speak at an event or even be Chairman. Get involved and make sure that people know you are there and ready to trade.

You may not be planning to leave a legacy within your profession or trade — that may be neither possible nor cost effective — but keeping a medium to high profile will not usually do you any harm and will keep your brand awareness high. Networking allows you the forum to influence your fellow business leaders and colleagues, both inside and outside your own profession or industry.

People always have and always will 'buy' people first.

Elevator pitch

You may remember the business marketing jargon of creating an *elevator pitch*. This is a short and punchy sales pitch to hit home your business message quickly and succinctly, in a way that the recipient will remember. The idea is that your business message should be something that rolls off the tongue in the time it takes an elevator to go from one floor to another, so that it's clear what you and your business do, and how you add value.

Mine is: we look after 'Woofies'! (Well-Off-Older-Folk), generally the over fifties age range, and offer pre-retirement, retirement, investment and inheritance tax planning. We also look after a select group of SMEs.

Maybe we should shorten our pitch to: we help people invest in their aspirations and life dreams.

That takes nine seconds in total to say. The best pitch I ever heard was from a party shop owner who simply says: '*We sell fun!*' Fabulous, you have my attention, which is the whole purpose.

You may want to criticise my 'pitch' in which case, please join the queue. However, I have not reviewed it for some years and now, for me, it is a time to adjust this to reflect the growth and maturity of our established brand.

Suggestions are most welcome — but before you do this, have a think about your own elevator pitch. If you do not have one yet, then prepare one. If you do have an elevator pitch, does it still reflect the transitional you to the forthcoming era? You may need an update.

When you next bump into the head of a target multinational, let's call her Mrs Decision-Maker, and you want to secure a meeting to discuss your latest idea, product or innovation —

bearing in mind that your business approach will probably be the tenth she has heard that morning — what are you going to say that will make a difference and allow you to win that next meeting?

Dancing girl

We had a young lady working for us during the summer months who was studying a Performing Arts degree. Katrina has great and admirable aspirations to become one of the greats on the boards in the West End. I asked her about her elevator pitch, and she looked back at me blankly. Life is about seizing opportunities when they arrive.

I asked: '*If you were at a party in London and, on leaving, got into a lift and there was the producer of a fabulous show, what would you say to him or her to make an impression?*' Remember, it might be your only chance to say, '*Hey, you need me in your shows!*' Katrina could see the point of having something ready to make that vital first impression.

Social media

> *Social media is just a buzzword until you come up with a plan.*
> — Anonymous

I have queried and still do question the value of some social media sites.

I am an early adopter of Twitter (@onlinefinancial) and I 'tweet' regularly, usually adding the hash-tag #financialthoughts at the end of any financial notes. Considering myself as merely a minor 'Twitterati', I have over 2,250 followers and am regularly 're-tweeted'. I enjoy the continued interaction, although I can confirm that I do not believe we have directly won any business from the messages deployed. I am not really in it for that.

Some people struggle with the spontaneity of Twitter, not knowing what to write that will be interesting and deliver the messages they want to convey. No one wants to know what you have had for breakfast or that it's raining where you are.

'Cheating' in this twitter context is not always a bad thing. If you struggle to stay within the 140 character limit, then sit down one evening (preferably with a nice glass of something) and write out 50 to 100 'tweets' that are interesting and relevant to your business/environment. Then feed in just two a day, marking the ones you have used so you don't accidentally repeat yourself. There are now systems designed to help you with this.

Add a relevant Twitter *hash-tag* (such as #financialthoughts in my case) to your message to allow people to follow your business theme, and away you go. As a minimum, this will allow you to be involved in this social media and will get you into the swing of things.

Do not forget to add a 'Follow us on Twitter' option (amongst others) on your website. It at least shows you are being in touch with modern techniques and, more importantly, communicative.

I have had less success with other major social media sites, which I find more time consuming than valuable, and have reduced my teams business time 'spend' on these to concentrate elsewhere more profitable. This is probably more about me than about their service, and possibly indicates that I can be a bit of a dinosaur in some internet-based areas.

Pick your preferred site(s), interact well on them, but have a presence on the other high-profile sites as well. You can usually link them if you connect accordingly.

Do these communication or marketing points add tangible business value? Perhaps not, but I am sure they will positively raise your profile and the work you want noted. I would rather be involved in social media than not. These options certainly do not *detract* from our business. This should be the case for you as long as it is well managed.

Also, as the demographics of the UK change and the older generation, like me, make way for younger aspirational folk, the real value of this media may come more to the fore in business and commerce. Again, it's a changing environment and a way of communicating that did not exist a few years ago. Not being involved, I think, is not an option because future generations will see this as the norm.

Not so long ago, people eyed with suspicion those new-fangled mobile telephones that were the size of breeze-blocks. Social media will be viewed the same way in a decade. Be involved, or get a nominated team member to be involved, in social media on behalf of your enterprise.

Going full circle

In the mid-1980s my father was retired early from a High Street bank from his role as Bank Manager. His work was strong, he had a good head for business and he still had plenty of energy — so his subsequent consultancy business was a success. His leaving was part of an overall realignment strategy. The plan for the UK banking company as a whole was to streamline, introducing new technologies which could reduce and replace man-hour requirements, as the bank correctly strove for efficiencies and greater margins of profitability. My father's agreed exit was at the start of this efficiency drive and it progressed over the next decade or so.

After this decade and a subsequent one, a 'new' marketing plan was introduced: the wild innovation of providing good service by re-introducing real Bank Managers who really could help with customers' banking needs. I chuckle at the thought of the circle closing, but it is of interest to note that, in this example, the way forward comes from the past.

Likewise, you may be aware that in Japan, their 'latest' business communication technology focuses on using . . . a Fax! I thought the last of these machines had been consigned to the scrap-heap in the late-1990s, my office being one of the last bastions and museum of such an artefact. However, it is just another example of technology going full circle.

When you are looking at innovation, product lines or sales initiatives, you may find that, as the pantomime catchphrase goes: *It's behind you!*

Remember to take a look at what the past can teach you for the future.

> *Who controls the past, controls the future;*
> *who controls the present, controls the past.*
> — George Orwell

Protecting your intellectual property

Some of you who have read my other business books will know that I am an advocate of protecting the intellectual property of a company at every point. This invaluable preparation was prior to my company's trademark dispute noted in Chapter Six. To some, their brand is not important, but to others, it embodies the real value within the business. I would always recommend that you secure the intellectual property and branding assets that you would hope to sell in the future.

As an example, if you own a brand name, make sure where possible that you also hold:

- The limited company registration (even if you are a partnership, the company can be maintained as a dormant entity)
- The website domain name (both .com and .co.uk, or more)
- Own the trade mark, both for the name and the logo.

Having finished a trade mark dispute that lasted almost twenty months, which took significant money, energy, angst and intellect to resolve, I realise the importance of this process. Having been tested in this way, the initial process we undertook to secure the points above proved to be invaluable. The challenge was exactly that: *challenging*.

Time, planning and effort moved on. Did I win? As in divorce, I do not think there *are* any real winners; just a compromise ensuring that each party does not destroy or encumber the other's business any further.

As your brand grows, take advice on protecting it now.

Website wording

Have you ever checked who might have plagiarised the text of those carefully written words on your website? Imitation may well be the highest form of flattery — but never when it comes to your business. There is always the risk that another entity may be trying to pass themselves off as your company, or worse.

There are websites that allow you to check this very issue, for example www.copyscape.com. Take a moment to have a look at this detail. We have certainly found it to be quite revealing, with one site even having our pictures on it! A quick solicitor's letter soon resolved this position.

I hope these notes have allowed you to question the security of your business brand name, and the goodwill value that you have built up and hope to sell at some point. The name you have is yours to lose if you don't protect it. Ignore these issues at your own cost.

> *Many of the things you count don't count.*
> *Many of the things you can't count, really count.*
> — Albert Einstein

Prams, toys and an occasional lob

I have spent all my working life in UK financial services.

First of all, complying with regulation forms a significant proportion of the financial services role, mixed in with obeying tax rules and requirements. This part is mainly tedious, but it has its moments.

Secondly, part of the role is understanding clients' needs and the motivations and emotions underlying that need. This means effectively *getting under the skin* of your client to really understand them — rather than guessing why they are at the point they are in their lives, and negotiating why they should sign on the dotted line to solve their problems and aspirations. It is a privilege to share these thoughts and planning with them.

These two points do not always sit comfortably with each other, because when you are dealing with people's emotions, you will not always get it right. People are complicated; in sharing their innermost thoughts about the serious issues of life, they can feel exposed. Getting it wrong can lead to complaints, which flies in the face of regulation. Too many complaints can be a sign of poor selling practices.

An employer once suggested that too *few* complaints indicated that you were not stirring the inner feelings of a client in your negotiations to get the most from an advice interaction, and ultimately make a sale. For me, at the time, this was the balance the financial adviser needs to find between retaining client trust and maximising sales promotion.

Of these, the former 'sales promotion' can be less profitable for everyone concerned in the medium to longer term. Negotiation is an art.

When running an enterprise, interactions or negotiations between clients, companies and associates will at times lead to heated debates and even conflict. Occasionally, this might mean that you 'throw your toys out of your pram' on a point of emotion, logic, principle or all of these combined. Contrary to what you might suppose, this can achieve a greater authority, because you have stood firm for something you believe in for you, your business and its future. Many will applaud you for being assertive at such times, and for maintaining standards and principles.

Whatever you do, do not have too many such tantrums or you could get a reputation for being puerile if you do not get your way. I witnessed this recently. The director concerned made themselves look incapable of managing even standard business negotiations without making themselves look unprofessional. At such times everyone involved walks away with a bitter taste in their mouth and they will guide their business away from any future involvement with that business or individual.

As you mature as an SME owner/director, arrogance can set in, leaving you with an unrealistic sense of confidence that your business is robust and above reproach. One well known (and now failed) retail chain found this out when its owner described his company's products as 'crap'! The subsequent fall-out speaks for itself.

Think about each transaction, negotiation and its consequences before deciding to stand firm on an issue. It might work, or it might just back-fire.

Snooping on the competition

You will know who your biggest competitors are. They will know about you. They will be ever changing and evolving and it is always good to keep an eye on them to see which way they want to take the same market that you compete in. The internet affords this opportunity.

I sometimes muse that the internet seems to have been created purely for Esther, my wife, who is also a Civil Engineer.

She can extract information from the World Wide Web that I would not have believed existed. All freely available (if you know where to look) and above board, the internet is a window to be used and interrogated. Every topic, within reason, has a way of revealing all its information, allowing Esther to piece together a dossier on her chosen target.

There are numerous excellent websites designed specifically to allow you to snoop around for information that some may hope would not be publicly available. Every company or business has a 'foot-print'; it's up to you to find its extent, if of interest.

Amongst others, examples of these include *www. snoop4directors.co.uk* or *www.company-director-check. co.uk*. Another good site we use is Companies House, at *www. companieshouse.gov.uk*. This website allows you to buy a set of previous year's accounts for a business at a small amount each time. If you really want to keep costs down, you could buy every *other* year's accounts and end up effectively paying £3 for six years' information.

This is useful for all manner of reasons. You might want to:

- Look at the financial strength of a business.
- Confirm the year the business actually started trading, rather than the year it was incorporated. Most people can register a company name for a cost of around £75 to £100, but this does not necessarily mean they are trading by that time.
- Confirm they are meeting their regulatory reporting requirements in a timely fashion. If this is not the case, it could be an indication of their overall administrative prowess or attention to detail having flaws. (The

Companies House website is very helpful for this and other information.)

- Confirm that the company is still trading, especially if it claims it has had consistent use of a trade mark.

Snooping on you

Knowledge is power.
— Sir Francis Bacon

Internet tools, such as www.statcounter.com or Google Analytics (website research tools to tell you who has been looking at your site, for how long and which pages) can be useful to see who may be undertaking some due diligence on your company before contacting you.

Being aware of what the situation is with a competitor or a service provider (over and above the sales bravado that you may have received) is always worthwhile, to confirm or clarify another party's true trading position and possible intentions.

All of the data noted here does not take long to collect, around five minutes if you know what to research. The real insight it provides is significant and can provide you with the gift of the upper hand in some negotiation situations.

Your Business Planning

🕐 Have you trade-marked your brand and logo because you have grown its real value? Who can you talk to who can help you?

🕐 How do you plan your business networking? And monitor its outcomes?

🕐 Are you coordinating this with your team to get the most value from it?

🕐 Does your business have a social media policy?

🕐 When was this last reviewed? How do you get value?

🕐 When is the last time you reviewed and renewed your website?

🕐 Who delivers this marketing and are they the right person for the role?

🕐 Do these marketing and networking plans or policies combine together well for maximum effect?

🕐 Do they reflect the dynamism you anticipate into the future?

🕐 Have you snooped for information *on your own business* to see what others can find out about your company?

Chapter Ten: Excited by the future?
You should be!

If you are ready for the future, you will need to ask some simple, but nevertheless challenging questions:

- Where has your business come from?
- Where is your company now?
- Where do you want it to be in the future?
- What is the target date to achieve this renewed objective?

It is as simple as these four questions, although each will take thorough and calculated planning before you have the answers.

So often now, I hear the need from many dynamic and determined business owners to grow. The planning and implementation that occurs in the next twelve months will make all the difference, as we move out of recession and into prosperity. It is going to take focus and hard work — nothing new to you.

Now is the time to set your business proposition straight to outperform your competitors in the future. There are many examples of this approach being successful in the past, with some current well-known household names coming to the fore from lowly beginnings as the economy emerged from recession.

> *The best way to predict the future is to create it.*
> — Peter Drucker

Every company and partnership has to start from the beginning, develop and mature, and your business is no different. It is just a question of how far you want to take it. The sky's the limit, if you have the will, intellect, drive and determination.

Keeping commercial focus now will be more important than it ever has been before, as many companies evolve and transform from survival mode to aspirational acceleration. Focusing on the end game should be a key priority in your new re-ignited growth programme.

Focusing on the end game

Starting with the end in mind is the culture of any good business, whether one is thinking about a product line, brand or service as a whole.

I have to admit that when I first started in business, decades ago, I struggled with this philosophy. This was mainly because I was still moving up the managerial 'food chain', and because systems, processes, meetings, notes, legislation, regulation and everything else seemed to merely clutter the message of what was trying to be achieved. I am sure this sounds familiar. I sometimes still refer to these disturbances as *noise*, usually drowning out the true message. Most people reading this will know how easy it can be to get deafened away from the path of growth.

For example, if you want to build a house on a particular site, it takes a lot of planning, time, money and negotiation before you can finally put the key in the door and move in. The process is done in stages with a suitably completed dwelling as the final production outcome.

The same applies to any tangible or non-tangible commodity being produced. This might mean anything from arranging the drawing of a valuable pension, to selling a pair of glasses, or even producing a car or a tin of sweets. The delivery of the end product is the goal and the target, on time, on budget and with a suitable profit margin.

Efficiency and volume

Each individual outcome is an end product, and it is the *efficiency* and *volume* of how you get there which will create corporate profits, assuming that you got your original business model right. (If you did not, I think it might be too late to be reading this book.)

Markets move on with time. What was profitable in the past is not necessarily so in the future. As we have noted, this is why so many businesses fail on the way out of recession. The production and sales of CD's provide a reasonable example and testament to this situation. As I have suggested before, standing still, in fact, means going backwards. History shows that inflation has never stood still for long and neither does commerce.

At this time of looking forward, investment in technology and systems to produce what you do now more efficiently, at greater volume, and with lower costs, has to be a great objective. Investment in your team and your people is just as important, if not more so.

Look at these points in your Company.

Vision of the future

Do you remember a time when it was considered that you really had 'arrived' once your business had a brochure? And then, as times changed, you were at the cutting edge of business communication by having a website. How modern! And with it you had an email address.

I am sure you will have thought about putting QR codes on your business cards that may direct smart phones to your website, or even better, to your own App. (This pre-supposes that you now *have* an App.)

In their time, each of these was at the very front of the change curve of business communications. Where next? The reality is that, like business, *you* need to be ready to embrace new communication techniques and modes as they become available. Whatever you do, make it easy for other companies, business leaders and end users of your product to find and communicate with you.

> *The rewards in life go to those who are willing to give up the past.*
> — Anonymous

Why just a Supermarket Sweep?

When you go to the supermarket you currently have the option of purchasing goods by running them through the till, assisted by the checkout assistant or by the use of a serve-yourself scanner. You are likely to have seen these in most large food retailers, allowing you to pack and pay promptly on exit.

There is no reason why this principle should not be extended to general High Street type shopping; scanning purchases from a range of retailers, that can be downloaded at home to create a shopping list that can then simply be submitted and delivered to your home.

With QR codes, contactless payment systems and other such technologies becoming standard practice, I see this inevitably becoming standard trading practice. It's a simple business opportunity waiting for you to embrace soon. But it is change and has to be embraced.

I am sure your office computer, even with its flat screen, will be replaced by tablets and other computer-driven devices soon. Be ready for these innovations as they will change the way individual companies do business in the future, whichever field they are involved in.

Putting your strategy together

I hope that this book has inspired you as the leader of your enterprise to take a few moments to step back and to reflect, dissect and interrogate, compare and contrast, reconstruct and, finally, focus and re-engage with vigour on your business!

How will you do this?

Reflect

- How have you and your business got to where you are now?
- Are you on target?
- Was your journey worth the reward?
- With the end in mind, are you still on course as part of your growth trajectory?
- Had the past recession not occurred, would your current position be any different? How?

Dissect and interrogate

- What would you have done differently if your crystal ball had nudged you to make changes?
- Do old Board minutes reflect the direction you still want to follow?
- What's changed and what is going to have to change, to be ready for the boom years?
- What cost savings could be made if you were being ruthless?
- Is your product or service still the dynamic model that you launched? Does your product or service need a review or fresh redesign?
- Is a client or end user survey appropriate now for your growth plans? What would it find?

Compare and contrast

- Who is your main competitor and what do they do that competes with you, whether successfully or unsuccessfully?
- Which way is your industry or trade or profession moving? Are there any new and interesting trends?

- What new techniques could you apply that would save costs or increase your products' reach?
- Is a *scope of economy or scale* available to your product or service line?

Reconstruct

- What changes can you introduce and effect now to move your business forward?
- Is your product or service range right? Should it be streamlined or even better, extended? How?
- What challenges will this change have in the short, medium and long term?
- Why these and how will you overcome or prepare for them?

Focus and re-engage

- Are you ready to reconfirm your belief in your corporate success?
- How will you communicate your vision and change process to your team and end users?
- Engage your team in the end goal. Do they understand and buy into it?
- Do it now. The end of the recession will not wait for you!

The expectations of life depend upon diligence; the mechanic that would perfect his work must first sharpen his tools.
— Confucius

Competition

I believe that other businesses, companies and practices will be considering the real opportunities ahead right now. Their lists and their process will be different to yours. We are all different, but the end game of growth will be the same target and objective.

Be assured, the economy will lift itself; it is just a case of where you want to take your place in the new growth era. The notes above provide you with a framework to investigate where you are and to encourage you to disengage (only for a short review period) from your day-to-day concerns in order to focus on what you and your business really want to achieve. You may want to take a few days off to accomplish this strategy planning, or do it one week in the evenings over a glass of wine perhaps. Do whatever suits your style, but whatever you do, make sure you do it now.

Enjoy the journey

I have enjoyed preparing the text for this book. It has allowed me to come away from our business 'coal-face' for long enough to concentrate on what our businesses need to change in order to ride the forthcoming prosperity curve. It would not be sensible to preach such business planning without using it myself!

The process has allowed me to revisit many ideas, initiatives and historical experiments, planning and outcomes, to put them to our advantage. I am pleased to say that we are closer to our renewed target than I had anticipated — but this does not mean that strategic changes will not be made. They will. These will be purposefully challenging and, on laying down my writing pen, I will address each one, and address them now.

I do not want to miss out, and neither should you!

Are you really ready?

It is lonely at the top when you run a business. Being the boss was never going to be easy. I am sure that you are not looking for pity. It is another 'p' word you will be searching out: profit. Even when you aspire to move from S (small) to M (medium) enterprise and on again to a larger corporation, commerce takes few prisoners, and you will aim to be at the top of your trade, business or profession at all times.

You did not start your company to make friends. You did it to make it a success, to provide income and to gain capital value when you are ready. Stay true to your course.

> *Good business leaders create a vision, articulate the vision, passionately own the vision, and relentlessly drive it to completion.*
> — Jack Welch

Do it now

Now is the time. What you do in the next twelve months may make all the difference in ten years' time, as you ride the recession curve out to real economic prosperity.

The world will not stand still and being innovative and energetic now will make all the difference. I anticipate that there will be various points in this book that will have challenged your existing thinking, and issues that ask you to take stock of where you are and where you want to be. There are many positive words sprinkled over the text of the pages, but also applied thinking and ideas, to help you plan your growth trajectory and the realistic ways this can be achieved.

Shared experience

Each of our business journeys will have been different, but we will have shared many experiences, situations, frustrations, angst and success as well. Our greatest success may have been simply to have survived the recession at all.

Our future is for growth

I also believe our greatest shared challenge is yet to come: to use the spring-board that is our respective established companies to jump to the next level of enterprise success. In the economic cycle that we share, many directors and executives would rather be out of the incubator and ready to capitalise on the work that has gone before, than being a new company start-up. To some extent, I agree with this sentiment: this next short period is the best, if not the only, opportunity we will see for the next decade or so for those enterprise leaders that are ready and prepared to thrive in a way that they have never enjoyed before.

Ready now?

As the back page of this book asks: *Are you and your business ready?* Only you will know the answer to this question. Time will tell if you are right, but whatever you do, do not miss this, possibly once in a lifetime, opportunity to make sure that you have reviewed and implemented changes to your company to ensure you are really prepared.

Prosperity and opportunity lie ahead in the business change curve of the global economy. It is just a question of how much of this growth opportunity you and your enterprise want.

See you at the winning line!

Your Business Planning

🕐 What are your main targets that you can set in the next twelve months that can be achieved in the next five years? Why these targets?

🕐 Have you mapped the time each agreed target should take?

🕐 How will you compare and contrast these targets to make sure they are being as effective as they could be?

🕐 Why these time frames? Can they be brought forward?

🕐 Which direction do you think your competitors will move? Why?

_____

_____

_____

_____

🕐 How are you going to build a six monthly review into your program to meet the targets you have set?

_____

_____

_____

_____

🕐 If you could name one thing you will do differently from now on to achieve your required outcomes, what would it be?

_____

_____

_____

_____

🕐 Do you and your team *believe* that your business will be successful into the future?

_____

_____

_____

_____

⏱ Are you and your business ready for prosperity, growth and eventual sale?

Epilogue

Before I sat down to write this book, with the belief that it really is 'Time to Grow', I asked myself:

⏱ *What makes this one different from any other book?*

When an aspiring business can no longer be called a 'start-up', but has yet to realise its maximum potential, it can be a challenge to acquire informed opinion, guidance and shared experience.

Nobody needs reminding about the economic gloom caused by the recession. This book focuses on ideas, reminders and motivational thoughts and their entrepreneurial leaders, to re-ignite and re-engage the growth phase of mothballed business plans.

Now is the time for business owners and directors to seize the opportunity that lies before *their* businesses. The decisions they make in the near future, I believe, will influence the outcome of their success in years to come.

⏱ *Why now?*

- Because, within the next twelve months, the recession really will be over and commerce will resume its journey towards prosperity.
- Reminding yourself as a business leader of ideas, theories, objectives and targets in idea-sized notes will inspire you to take action.

⏱ *Who am I writing this book for?*

- Aspiring SME directors and partners
- Wannabe business owners
- CEOs of existing and maturing businesses and charities
- Those leaders that have 'plateaued' within their company and want to break free from the shackles of the recession, pushing forward with vigour and renewed enthusiasm.

⏱ *How can I make such a dry subject inspirational?*

Sharing experiences, mistakes, successes, ideas, reminders and opinion allows you as the reader to take from this book energy, and I hope dynamism, to make a real difference to the decisions and directions that business leaders will take in the next year.

I just tell it like it is.

Resources

- Film *Kinky Boots* by Deane & Firth (2005)

- Dr Amelia Fletcher, Chief Economist, The Office of Fair Trading, 'The impact of price frames on consumer decision making', May 2010

- Herzberg's motivation-hygiene theory, Frederick Herzbergs 'The motivation to work' 1959

- Kahneman & Tversky, 1979, *Prospect Theory*

- Elton Mayo's Hawthorne Experiments, Harvard, 1927-1932

- Office of National Statistics, Divorce Statistics 2011, Published December 2012

- Panzar and Willig (1977, 1981), John C. Panzar and Robert D. Willig (1977). 'Economies of Scale in Multi-Output Production', Quarterly Journal of Economics

About the author

Keith Churchouse BA (Hons), FPFS,
Certified Financial Planner®,
ISO22222 Personal Financial Planner

Having worked in the financial services industry for over a quarter of a century, and qualified to a high level within UK retail financial services, Keith set up Chapters Financial Limited with Esther Dadswell in 2004, a Chartered Financial Planning company in Guildford, Surrey. The company is authorised and regulated by the Financial Conduct Authority.

Keith also completed a BA (Hons) degree in Financial Services in 2007 with Napier University and became a Fellow of the Personal Finance Society in December 2007. In 2008, using Standards International, he was the fourth person in the UK to achieve ISO 22222 Personal Financial Planner status, the British Standard for Personal Financial Planners.

Taking an avid interest in his local Surrey based business community, Keith became chairman of the Guildford Business Forum in 2011 and is also Trustee to two excellent local charities, including Headway Surrey. At the time of writing, he is also Apprentice Ambassador to Guildford College, and maintains various directorships of local companies.

Keith has made regular expert comment in the local and national press and has frequently been interviewed on money matters on BBC local radio over the last eight years.

In 2010, Keith detailed his twenty-five years' experience in retail financial services in his first book, *Sign Here, Here and Here! . . . Journey of a Financial Adviser.*

He has an active social media presence and can be found on Linkedin.com and Twitter as @onlinefinancial.

In addition, he tries to have a life outside work, and enjoys writing books, art, keeping fit by cycling, scuba diving and classic cars and scooters.

designed by

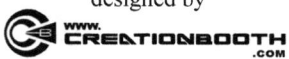

www.ingramcontent.com/pod-product-compliance
Lightning Source LLC
Chambersburg PA
CBHW060027210326
41520CB00009B/1036